Lessons From
Spirit

Trina Brown

First published by Busybird Publishing 2023

Copyright © 2023 Trina Brown

ISBN:
Paperback: 978-1-922954-87-9
Ebook: 978-1-922954-88-6

This work is copyright. Apart from any use permitted under the *Copyright Act 1968*, no part of this publication may be reproduced, stored in a retrieval system or transmitted in any form or by any means, electronic, mechanical, photocopying, recording or otherwise, without the prior written permission of Trina Brown.

The information in this book is based on the author's experiences and opinions. The author and publisher disclaim responsibility for any adverse consequences, which may result from use of the information contained herein. Permission to use any external content has been sought by the author. Any breaches will be rectified in further editions of the book.

Cover design: Busybird Publishing

Layout and typesetting: Busybird Publishing

Busybird Publishing
2/118 Para Road
Montmorency, Victoria
Australia 3094
www.busybird.com.au

Contents

Acknowledgements	1
Preface	3
Chapter One I Knew A Man	7
Chapter Two Magpie Family	20
Chapter Three My Brother My Blood	35
Chapter Four Photographs and Memories	46
Chapter Five A Gift Like No Other	54
Chapter Six He Who Hunts	72
Chapter Seven A Mother's Wish	82
Chapter Eight No Goodbyes	97
Chapter Nine Life Declined	109

Chapter Ten
Animal Friends   119

Chapter Eleven
This Is Me   128

Chapter Twelve
Life Is For Laughter   139

Chapter Thirteen
My People in Spirit   151

Chapter Fourteen
Lessons to Learn   161

About the Author   173

ACKNOWLEDGEMENTS

I give heartfelt thanks to a group of people who are always by my side. My guides in spirit, My People. You have helped me become the person I am today and I will always be grateful to you. Each one of you have taught me so many lessons, too many to mention here. But you have ultimately all taught me, with great understanding, patience and empathy, that it is okay to be me. You have shown me that love has no bounds and that one world can interact with another. And to do this, we must trust and listen to those that hold the wisdom of many lifetimes. I dedicate this book to My People in spirit as you have shown me the greatest truth: that life is always worth living. And when our physical bodies cease to live, we continue to live on in the world of spirit, always embraced by a love that holds no bounds.

I would like to thank my children for being such wonderful human beings and supporting me in everything I do. Rory and Taegan, you will always be my greatest accomplishment and I love you both dearly. Thank you for choosing me to be your mumma and making me feel blessed each and every day.

Rusty, you are with me every day encouraging me with my work as a clairvoyant medium and also encouraging me to keep writing. But you do so much more than just that. You support me in any way you can and love me for exactly who I am. Even when sometimes living with this little clairvoyant medium can become a little weird. You make me laugh, you listen to my sometimes crazy words and show me I am loved. You are my rock, my love and my best friend. I'm very blessed to have you in my life.

To the clients who have allowed me to write about their experiences with their loved ones in spirit. Thank you for trusting me to write of those moments that have often been so hard to live through. I admire your strength, courage and grace in facing such difficult times. But I also know you have gained something special – the belief that we do go on in the world of spirit after the physical body has ceased to live. And, that the bond of love is greater than the ending of a physical life.

To my extended family, friends, clients and students. Thank you for allowing me to be me and supporting me in all I do.

Thank you to Sue Sheerman, for being the beautiful person you are and creating the artwork on my cover.

Finally, I would like to thank Busybird Publishing for helping me throughout the publishing of this book. You have all been so wonderful throughout this entire process.

Preface

Everyone we come into contact with throughout our life has the potential to teach us many different things. It is my belief that each of us has been given a soul. To me, the soul is that part of you that lives on after the physical body dies. It stores all the individual life lessons that you have been given in this life, past lives and future lives. Some people will teach you at a soul level and it is my belief that your family and those closest to you will be your greatest teachers.

In this book, I have recounted some of my own life experiences and the lessons some of my precious family have taught me as I travel through life. My guides in spirit have also taught me a multitude of lessons and have been included, as they have been with me for my lifetime. Some of my beautiful clients who have lost loved ones have given their permission to also share their stories, to show even in our deepest loss, we learn that there is hope. Life is certainly filled with lessons that are sometimes hard, but those lessons teach us more deeply about ourselves.

It is my belief that we are often put in particular family groups to learn lessons, so we develop in character and wisdom. These lessons can be quite difficult as we experience them. But, as you learn to delve into them deeply, you can often see why you needed to go through the different experiences and interact with the individuals you meet throughout your life. Often, significant self-growth is achieved while doing this and your life path constantly changes. We all have choices, so it depends on which choice you choose as to which path your life may follow.

Each day we live, there is the opportunity to learn the mysteries of why we have been born onto this earth. We can evolve as an individual if we choose to look deeper into those experiences life hands out to us.

We are each a soul travelling within a human body. On our soul's journey we often discover there are many different layers to each event we experience in life. How we react to those events or experiences are varied and completely unique to each individual.

I believe that we continue to die and be born again until we have mastered the lessons of the soul. I have actually seen some of my past lives. But they have only been shown to me to help me uncover some of the things I need to understand about myself in this life. In seeing these past lives, I often discover soul lessons that have occurred and may still be occurring in this current life.

Think of your life on Earth as a classroom. Once you enter this classroom, how much knowledge you gain is your responsibility. Just like your teachers here on Earth can help teach you lessons, they can only show you as much as you wish to learn. It's up to you whether to engage in the lessons being taught. They cannot fully teach someone who chooses not to learn. And just like entering a school, there will be good days and bad. There will be times you will excel and other times you just can't master the lesson.

If you can, focus on the lesson of tolerance for a moment and think about how you relate to tolerance in your life today. Now I can tell you I have great tolerance for most things and people. But there are times when I may be around someone who is constantly loud and overbearing, to the point they have no regard for other points of view. I can sometimes feel my tolerance waiver and my mind starting to judge in these situations and I know I still have to study the lesson in more depth. Just imagine how many actual soul lessons there are to tolerance. I'm pretty sure there are hundreds, if not more.

I ask you to try and not see your life so much as a series of arduous tests. Instead, I ask you to see your life as a wonderful journey where you learn to become completely involved with every experience that comes your way. And in doing so, you become the best possible version of yourself. That in itself, is one of the most important lessons of life here on Earth.

Chapter One

I Knew A Man

I knew a man,
A very gentle, humble man.

Brown eyes so dark and deep.
Your smile, dear old Dad, I will always keep.

Many times, I watched you struggle,
Life's hardships you tried so hard to juggle.

I watched you, silent. Quietly thinking and twirling your hair.
As a child I understood how much your mind could not bear.

A glass or two to keep you going.
Time spent outside, a garden you were always growing.

Hands that could create the most beautiful artwork or deliver a punch.
A hot pot of stew made with love you placed in front of us for lunch.

A man sitting outside knitting clothes for my dolls.
Of laughter and spiders running up your arms when beer took its toll.

Quiet breakfasts spent together, you drinking your beer.
Always making sure I didn't leave for school without some
sort of cheer.

'You Are My Sunshine' forever sings in my mind and heart.
Oh, how brilliant my dad, you were with your art.

I think of a heart so full and sublime.
A heart that stopped beating forever in time.

A treasured picture lost you drew for me of horse and foal.
Knowing in my heart your death would teach my soul.

I think of your dark brown eyes and gentle loving smile.
Of how the universe made you my dad so I had the courage
to walk so many miles.

So many memories a daughter holds in her heart and mind
Of a loved and loving father that I'm so proud to say was mine.

It is often said that a father is the first true love a daughter will experience and all others that follow will have to live up to that love. I think that is so very true.

My father was a very gentle man who never raised his voice. He was quiet and unassuming. With regards to work, he was a jack of all trades and a master of none, picking up jobs as a labourer or hay carter most of the time.

But there was one thing he was brilliant at, and that was drawing. He would spend time bent over paper with pencil or pen in hand and before long, the most incredible images would appear on the page. He had this wonderful gift of being able to capture an image through his artwork. It didn't matter if he was using pen, pencil or paint, the detail in his drawings was incredible. He had a gift, but unfortunately, he never truly used it to help himself in his life. Realistically, he hadn't been given the opportunity to do this. And yes, he was my first love. He would later teach me to strive to become the very best version of myself.

My father didn't talk much about his upbringing. I think there was just too much pain for him to talk openly about his childhood. His mother had died at thirty-five in tragic circumstances and my father and his brothers weren't allowed to attend her funeral. I know the loss of his mother left a huge scar on his heart. My father's mother had a very hard life, coping with the boys as well as a husband who could be a major problem. I never had the privilege of meeting her in person, but I do have the honour of having her name as my second name. And at different times, I have talked to her in spirit. My dad's father died at forty-five and really wasn't there for the family as he was often out drinking. As I was growing up, my dad never actually mentioned his father's drinking problem. I later found out through relatives that he was an alcoholic who could become aggressive when he was drunk.

Not long after the death of his mother and due to his father never being home, he was given twenty pounds from the aunts he was living with and told to go make his way in the world. He was fourteen, only a child when those who were looking after the children decided he must leave, as they could not look after all the boys. I actually only found out about these details a few years back, when my uncle had become ill and I was talking to him about the family and Dad's upbringing.

So, Dad travelled to country Victoria and eventually met the love of his life, my mother. But somewhere along his journey through life, he too followed the path of his father, and drinking became part of his life. It would become the way he would face all the hardships he had to deal with. But unlike his own father, I never saw him once get violent when drinking. In fact, most of the time he just became more social and outgoing.

My father was a very good boxer. He taught me as a child how to hold my hands and stand correctly so I could defend myself.

I remember him saying, 'Hold your hands up near your face, sweetheart. Protect your head. Move those feet and dodge my punches.'

All of this was of course done with a grin on his face and a sparkle in his eyes as we sparred in our backyard.

And often he would gently clip my head and say, 'Uh oh, gotcha! Someone hasn't listened to dear old Dad.'

I'd giggle at his dramatic facial expressions, knowing full well he was joking with his daughter.

As I look back over his life, I've come to the realisation my father took up boxing not only because of the skill it involved, but to also release things he couldn't always come to terms with in his life. I think he realised it was better to use his frustration in a sport rather than physically take it out on the world like his own father did.

I remember him saying, 'Sweetheart, the only time we throw a punch is to defend ourselves. The moment a boxer punches outside a ring he is stupid and has already lost the fight.'

My dad was indeed a contradiction. One day he would be teaching me how to box and yet I have beautiful memories of him knitting my dolls clothes on my grandmother's front porch. I remember watching him knit, with my doll perched on my knee as I sat waiting patiently to see what he had made for her.

One day he got up abruptly and said, 'We will finish this inside, sweetheart.'

And as I followed him in, I saw my mother start to laugh and kid him about why he was coming inside. My father hadn't realised the time and didn't want the school kids walking past Gran's house to see him knitting, as it wasn't considered manly in those days.

Throughout my growing years, I saw him create the most delicious meals out of what seemed like an extremely sparse pantry. Although, I did turn my nose up when he offered me bread and dripping. I refused point plank to eat it, knowing full well it was basically left-over fat on a piece of bread!

He'd laugh and say, 'What's wrong with you? You mustn't be that hungry!'

I would watch him hunched over paper, pencil in hand, drawing the most incredible drawings. At times he showed me how to draw certain things. But seriously, all I managed to draw reasonably well was the redhead lady on a box of matches! I'm definitely not an artist like my dad.

But often those gifted hands of his would reach for the alcohol. Unlike he did with his pencil, I knew that alcohol was something he could not always put down. He would often be the source of our laughter as we watched the alcohol take its toll on his body. Memories of him singing 'You are My Sunshine' or 'Do What You Do Well' as he came in the door after a drinking session. Or trying to show us that spiders were not to be feared as he talked to large huntsman spiders he allowed to run up his arm. This happened every time my mother asked him to remove them from the house. My brothers and I would scatter, laughing both at his antics but also fearing the spider may land on us at any moment. My mother continued to scold him and shake her head because much to her dismay, he never made a quick exit with the spider. He tried to convince us the spider had every right to live in the house because he was catching insects. On the odd occasion I saw her grin as she shook her head. We all found it hilarious.

One time, I distinctly heard him in the distance coming home. He was singing at the top of his voice and all the dogs up the street were barking at his singing. There was a loud yelp and a dog howling, and I thought to myself, *What have you done, Dad?* He came in the door saying he just taught a dog a lesson.

When my mother asked what he had done, he replied, 'The dog was making too much noise, so I bit him on the ear. He's okay. He just needed to learn to be quiet.'

I couldn't help but chuckle at his logic, but I don't think my mum was that impressed by the look on her face.

My dad loved dogs, and we had many beautiful dogs as pets when we were growing up. As a young girl, I often loved to watch my father train a new pup that was to become a part of our family. He spent hours with them, teaching them obedience and manners. You could see the dog's love for him. My father never raised his voice. In fact, as children, we were never hit or treated with anything other than love. But on the odd occasion, as all pups do, they would chew shoes or take washing from the clothesline. You would see my father's eyes grow even darker than the deep brown they were. He would scold them and tell them how bad they were, and on the odd occasion chase them until they ran under the house. The dog instinctively knew it was in deep trouble and was trying to escape Dad's anger. But thankfully, that anger didn't last long and within a short time, the dog would be back at Dad's feet, with Dad telling it what a good boy it was and the dog affectionally licking his face.

My dad was a beautiful man, but yes, he was an alcoholic. He often found it hard to find work, and any time not spent at work was replaced with drinking. As a result, we often didn't have enough money to pay our bills or have the necessities of life. But even when he did have work, drinking was still on his agenda.

As a young child having my abilities, I could often feel his pain and also know when he was about to go on a drinking bender. I would watch him deep in thought, twirling his hair around his finger as his mind went over and over his thoughts. I knew he was struggling, yet as a child had no idea how to help him. Then the beer bottle would appear, and I knew he had succumbed to the alcohol to numb the pain.

Time and time again, the alcohol would become the main priority in his life, yet I knew he loved us dearly. I often found it difficult to understand how a liquid could consume your mind so much that it became a source of necessity. You couldn't live without having it pass your lips. But I was a child. I didn't know how addiction could rule your life.

I only saw my father cry twice in my life. I had come home from school, and at this stage we lived in a pickers hut because we had been kicked out of a commission house as my parents hadn't paid the rent. Dad hadn't been working for a long time and the bills had piled up and my parents just weren't able to scrape the money together for rent. I had a makeshift bedroom in the hut, consisting of a single bed and bedside table and was cordoned off by a brightly patterned curtain. It wasn't much of a bedroom, but I didn't really mind the fact that I didn't have walls surrounding me.

As I rode up on my bike, I heard My People in spirit say, 'Little One, there is sadness in his heart today.'

I parked my bike against the hut and walked around the corner of the house and saw Dad sitting in a chair smoking a cigarette. I could feel his sadness and I silently watched him as he began to cry. I saw the tears fall down his face and I felt his depth of sorrow.

'What's wrong with him?' I asked My People in spirit.

'He has lost a friend, Little One.'

I backed away, knowing Dad wouldn't like me to see his tears, and waited for him to go inside. Later, Mum told me our black Labrador had been run over by a car. Dad loved this dog and spent every waking moment with the dog by his side. I understood now, he saw his dogs as his friends. He knew this dog had no judgement of him. The dog just loved him, just as he loved his dog.

The second time I saw my dad cry was when I was seventeen. I had decided I needed to get out of town and see the world. I was heading for Queensland, which in those days was a rite of passage.

I said goodbye to my mum and dad on our front lawn. I could feel his energy. He was very quiet, which always told me he was struggling with something in his mind. He hugged me and I felt his chest heave and a sob escaped and I knew he was crying. As he let me go, he brushed his face and stood with his hands in his pockets looking down at the ground, as he often did when he couldn't deal with things.

As I drove away, he looked up and smiled and waved. My dad had such a beautiful smile, but I saw his pain. His little girl was leaving, and I too could feel the tears stinging my eyes. He was the first man I ever loved and all those that were to follow had a hard task living up to this man I lovingly called my dear old dad.

I lived in Queensland for a year but as Christmas approached, I began to yearn for my family. I missed my friends and I knew I needed to be back with those that loved me. I had had enough adventure and even though I found it was a fantastic experience, my family ties were pulling at my heart strings.

I thought it would be a great idea to surprise my parents. So, I only told my aunt about my homecoming. I arrived home on 22 December and there were shrieks of surprise and laughter as I greeted Mum at the back door of our family home. But Mum explained unfortunately Dad had left earlier to do some hay carting because money was a little tight, as usual, and the extra cash was needed for Christmas.

I had been travelling for two days in a bus, so after a cup of tea and a chat with Mum, I went to lay down to get some rest. I didn't sleep much because I was excited about seeing my dad and brothers, but managed to rest my eyes at least.

Then I heard a loud knock at the front door. My mother began screaming. I rushed to my mother, shocked at her screams.

The police were at the door and all my mum could say was, 'Oh Trine, oh no, it's your father.'

I was confused, I didn't understand! I looked at the policemen for answers and asked them what was wrong, but they didn't say a thing. I looked back at Mum, and she seemed to be crumbling.

I asked again, 'What, Mum? Tell me what has happened.'

She answered in between sobs, 'He's dead. Your father's dead.'

The look of grief and disbelief on her face is etched deeply in my mind, even to this day. The love of her life, the man she had been married to for all those years. My father. He was dead.

Over the next few days, people came and went, offering their sympathies. It felt like I wasn't fully in my body. I felt like I was in a dream, a horrible nightmare. Then it was Christmas Eve, and the day of his funeral. To this day, I can't remember a great deal of his funeral apart from one moment when I saw my mother's look of confusion at the end of the service. They were walking her husband, my dad, out in his coffin. She sat stunned, not knowing what to do. She looked at me with such sadness, panic and confusion. I encouraged her to get up and after what seemed like such a long time, she rose, and we walked out of the church together.

I can't remember the eulogy, the songs, who was there or even entering the church. I can't remember him being placed in the earth. All I remember is my mother's face at that moment of intense grief. Years later, I researched where he was buried in the cemetery as I had no idea where his grave laid. The shock of his death was just too much for me to handle. To this day, I still grieve for my beautiful dad.

The weeks and months passed. I found it difficult to express how much his death had affected me. I couldn't understand why My People in spirit didn't tell me he was going to die. And I was also angry at my dad for letting me down. I thought, *How dare you die without seeing me! How dare you be so weak that you had to go without one more hello!*

I began to follow the path of my dad and his dad. I began to drink to dull the pain of his loss. Before long, I needed alcohol to make me feel happy. Yet as I woke sober, I would spiral into deep depression. I knew I was wasting my life with all the drinking, but I would still reach for it to comfort me, again and again. Each time I felt the heavy weight of grief I would succumb to the alcohol in the hope it would comfort me, or at least dull the pain I was feeling. But after quite a few drinks I would end up sobbing uncontrollably. I would then sink into a silent depression, a world where there was no talking, no want or need to converse with those around me. I became silent, just like my father, as I grappled with my demons.

My dad would visit me in my dreams, trying to get through to me as I wouldn't talk to him in spirit when he visited me. I was angry – so darn angry at him for leaving me here all alone. I had watched him many times as a child choose alcohol instead of facing reality, instead of being there for us. In my mind, in my grief, I thought he had again not thought of us and taken the easy way out. I felt him in spirit by my side many times, trying to help me, but I pushed him away. I was too angry at him to allow him to come close and help me.

One day I was on my lunch break and I saw a sign advertising a psychic. I was curious. I thought why not give it a go and see what my future holds? But really, I was mostly looking for help to get out of the lifestyle I had created in my grief. I went inside to find a thin, dark-haired lady with cards in front of her, smoking a cigarette. Smoke was filling the room and the smell took me aback. She smiled and asked me to sit.

She began to describe my life and the struggles I was going through. Then she described a man in spirit who was dark in skin tone, quiet and had a problem with alcohol. Then she lifted her finger and twirled her hair around her finger.

She looked at me and said, 'He would do this when he was deep in thought.'

The tears began to fill my eyes and gently roll down my face. She was describing my dad.

She leaned over and touched my hand, saying, 'He didn't want to leave you. It was his time, he had no choice.'

Now I was sobbing. I tried to compose myself but could not stop my tears.

She said, 'You have a gift, just like your father.'

I stiffened; she was wrong. My father was extremely gifted with his artwork. In a matter of minutes, he could replicate anything he saw onto paper with such intricate detail. Me? I couldn't draw a stick figure, let alone draw like my father. My jaw tightened and I wanted to leave. I wanted to get away from this woman. She was wrong.

'No,' she said, 'not the gift of drawing. You will help many people in the future. You will help these people come to terms with the loss of those they love. You see and hear your father. But you refuse to acknowledge him because you are angry with him for leaving.' She sat back and sighed. 'Just like your father, you have poison in your life. You cannot do what is needed unless you let go of this poison.' I knew she was talking about the alcohol. 'Do not follow your father's path. Do not destroy what you have been given by God.'

She explained he had been by my side each and every day since his death, but soon he must leave to help my brother. Immediately I panicked and thought, *No, please don't go, Dad. Please stay with me. I cannot do this on my own. I'm sorry I was angry; I didn't realise you didn't have a choice. I thought you had let me down, that you wanted to take the easy way out. I thought you had chosen to leave me.*

The lady could see my fear and distress at the thought of never seeing my father again.

'It's okay, he will return when you need him. But your brother will need him more soon. He loves you Trina, now go out and make his death the reason you live. Go out and show the people who you are, sweetheart. But remember, you cannot do this while you have poison in your body.'

I got up and walked out of the smoke-filled room, exhausted, my eyes swollen from crying. I was both saddened and elated at the same time. In my mind I thanked my dad and told him

I loved him dearly. Immediately he was at my side and I felt his love.

'I love you sweetheart; remember you are my sunshine. You can do anything you put your mind to. Don't be like me. Go out and become who you were born to be.'

The tears flowed again, and I sobbed uncontrollably. I didn't want to talk to anyone or see anyone while I processed what had just happened. I found a quiet place and sat. I just wanted to be with my dad. I just wanted to sit and feel his energy. To hear his voice and see his beautiful smile and deep brown eyes. And the wonderful thing is, I could. No, I would never again have him here in the flesh, but I could communicate with him in spirit. And I knew I was blessed to have this much of him.

My father's death was to be the catalyst to change my life. I knew now it was very important I looked at my life and how it needed to change so I could do what I was born to do. I had always been able to see, hear and feel Spirit. And in some way, I knew even from a very young age that I would work with Spirit in some capacity. But I had never thought about being a medium, someone who was a go-between for those in spirit and those left behind on Earth. But I also knew I needed to get my drinking and depression under control if I was going to take on the commitment of working with Spirit.

The day my father died, is still to this day, the worst day of my life. I was so excited to be home for Christmas and was looking forward to spending time with my family. Our family loved Christmas and all that comes with the festive season. But the universe had other ideas. As the years rolled on, I understood why my father's death was such an important part of why my life was to change.

There were many times when I was growing up that I thought to myself, *Why are you my dad? Why do you have to make everything so hard? Why is the drink more important than us?* But do you know what? I would not want any other dad in the world, because to me he was my world.

Christmas would be forever changed in my mind. Each year, I still feel the grief of losing a loved and loving father. But I believe my dad's soul gave me the most important gift I would ever receive. He gave me his death so I may learn to live fully. I believe my father gave me the greatest life lesson and that was to learn to use what the universe had given me at birth to create the best version of myself. And in doing so, to help others to see their path and prove to them that we do live on after death. But to do all this, I had to first experience the greatest loss of my life and then dig myself out of the grief and negativity that loss had created.

At birth, I was given the gift of being able to see life continues after death. My father's death showed me, I must learn to use this gift to help myself and others. His death would be the catalyst to make my life what it was always meant to be.

I see my father as being my soulmate. We often think of soulmates as being a romantic love, but that's not always the case. To me a soulmate is someone who teaches you the hardest lesson you will ever learn. I also believe we often meet as souls before we come to this earth plane and decide what each soul can teach another throughout their life. To me, my father's soul gifted me the most important lesson my soul could learn in this lifetime. What a wonderful, selfless lesson, given to a daughter from her loving father.

Chapter Two

MAGPIE FAMILY

One, two, three magpies nesting in a tree.
Please oh please magpies, don't you dare swoop me.

Illness shows its ugly head.
Battles to be faced with such strength, courage and dread.

Days rolled on and before long all I knew as family were gone.
Spirit has called them all home, no one to support me, now all alone.

I hear them sing, I see them fly, and I feel their love.
I now know my family has been watching me from above.

Along came Spirit, they saw my sorrow and gave me
the most beautiful gift.
Magpies once a fear and in the distance, now sitting with me to uplift.

One, two, three magpies and me.
Back together once again, yes, we are family.

When I was a young girl, I was absolutely terrified of magpies. Come spring, they seemed to be everywhere, ready to dive down and swoop me at any opportunity. They would often nest in the huge pine trees in front of my school and I would walk past thinking, *Please don't, please don't swoop me today.*

I remember vividly, one day walking to school and they attacked me without mercy. I could hear their wings as they flew down and swooped. They were in full attack mode! I started to run as fast as my little legs could go, sure in my mind they were out for my blood.

I hadn't even realised I was running home and not toward school. Until there I was at the front gate and my mother was looking at me with a look only a mother can give.

'What are you doing back home, Trine?'

Immediately I answered, 'I'm not going back, the magpies are going to swoop me.'

I was adamant, there was no way I was going back. But Mum was just as stubborn as her daughter and put her foot down.

'Yes, you are, Trina.'

I always knew I was in trouble when she used my full name rather than calling me Trine. I started to cry, as the thought of these horrible birds swooping down to peck my eyes out filled my mind. I was beside myself with fear.

Mum's eyes softened and she said, 'We will go together, I'm sure they won't hurt you. They are probably gone by now.'

She closed the gate and we began to walk, my little legs feeling weak as we came closer to the school. I began scanning the sky for any glimpse of these evil birds that I was sure were out for blood. But sure enough, my mum was right – they had gone. Or in my mind, they were waiting for my mum to disappear so they could resume their attack. She could see my fear and walked me right past the huge pine trees and into the safety of the school hallway.

I never forgot that day and I continued to be very wary of magpies for many years. I watched to see where they nested and of course avoided those areas at all costs.

Many years later, my mother owned a house with a very large and long front yard. Much to my disgust, she had befriended a family of magpies. Every year, these magpies would return and take residence in her trees and sit on her porch waiting for her to come out and sit with them. Often, she would have food to give them. She loved to just sit and talk to them, connecting with them at a level I was yet to understand.

When I came to visit, I would open her front gate and scan her yard to see where they were. Immediately I would start to get anxious at the thought of running the magpie gauntlet. In my mind it was a very long way to the sanctuary that was my mother's lounge.

As I made my way towards her front door, I walked quickly with my head down, hoping the magpies wouldn't notice me.

Often, I would hear my mum chuckle and she would call out, 'Trine, they are my maggies, they won't hurt you.'

Really? I didn't believe her. To me they were evil creatures that couldn't be trusted. But to get to my mum I had to run the magpie gauntlet … and I did! But do you know what? To my surprise, my mother's magpies never once swooped me in her yard. In fact, they often greeted me with lots of warbling as though they were greeting me and letting my mother know I was here to visit.

The years rolled on and before long I was watching my mother die from lung cancer. My mother had been diagnosed with Lupus years earlier and her cancer was a complication from that illness. She had not been in good health for many years. I had actually diagnosed her Lupus some years earlier, asking her to go to the doctor and tell him her symptoms were a form of Lupus.

I was by her side every step of the way, from diagnosis of lung cancer to when she took her last breath. It was an honour to be there for her. She was such a strong, supportive woman, my mum. Not one for a lot of affection, she didn't give lots of hugs or often tell you how much she loved you. But she was someone I always knew I could count on no matter what.

As her illness progressed, I became more and more aware of magpies showing up in unusual places. They always seemed to be there in the background. But then things seemed to change even more dramatically. I didn't see them as being quite so evil; they began to intrigue me. I watched them more closely and tried to understand why they were coming close without swooping.

Then one day I came to the realisation these birds were a part of my mother. They were connected to her energy, her spirit. In some way they were giving me messages about what was to come for her. I began to no longer fear them. In fact, I welcomed the unusual places they turned up to show me they not only supported my mother, but also me.

As my mother came to the end stages of her life, I spent many hours sitting at her side just talking and passing the time. I knew my mother was going to die. When she was first diagnosed, I had walked into her house and immediately been overcome by the smell of hospitals as I looked at my father's photograph. This was the first sign. Then I had a dream I was walking up to the front door of my mother's house and there were Native people lining my path as I walked. I could feel their sadness and support. I woke to tears streaming down my face. I knew this dream was preparing me to say goodbye.

I had asked My People in spirit when this would happen and they answered, 'When the bird that eats meat comes so close you can touch, and the heavens open, it will be near.'

I didn't understand their words at the time. But I kept them in my mind as I knew this was important information.

I didn't want my mum to die. But I also knew it was a privilege to be able to spend time with her and I wanted to spend as much time as I could with her.

Before long she could no longer be nursed at home and was taken to hospital, a place neither of us liked at all. I was known for fainting and becoming very anxious in hospitals due to a bad experience I had when I was younger. My mum, well she just hated them and would have preferred to be in her own home.

But I put on my big girl pants and each time I went into the hospital I asked my guides to walk with me and before long, I began to cope. Really, there was no other choice. There was no way I'd leave my mum to go through this alone. She was my rock. A person who would never let me down, no matter what. I wouldn't dream of letting her down. As her daughter, it was my privilege to give back all she had given me.

We talked and laughed, and I would massage her feet to relieve some of the pain associated with not being able to be mobile. Most of her illness was spent in a chair. She could breathe better when her body was upright and her body felt more comfortable. She always had a smile on her face when I came to visit.

She would greet me with, 'Hi Trine, how are you?' She was always one to put the wellbeing of others before her own problems.

I would often bring her in small treats to get her to eat and keep up her strength. A battered sea scallop and a few sips of a milkshake were her favourite. But due to the symptoms of her illness she would never be able to finish even the sea scallop.

One day, I sat down as she was sipping on her milkshake and went to begin massaging her feet. But immediately I was zapped by an electric shock. Both of us were surprised and a little shocked. But I laughed and tried to continue. Again, a shock ran through me as I touched her, the shock so strong I nearly lost my footing. We both laughed, but I wondered what was going on. Mum then proceeded to tell me of a dream she had of her Aunt Ruth and Uncle Stan coming to help her pull down a house.

She asked me what it meant and I immediately said, 'Oh that's lovely, they are by your side in spirit, Mum.'

But I knew the dream really meant they were getting her ready to pass on from this world to the next, the world of spirit.

For a week or more, I continued to get zapped by my mother each time I touched her. Finally, I asked my guides in spirit why was this happening. They explained her body was weakening and her energy was moving closer to spirit. They advised me to think of my feet before I touched her and to protect my energy more so I wouldn't be affected as much. Their advice worked, and I was no longer zapped.

My days became about my mum. I would wake up thinking about her and wonder if she would be okay until I managed to get to her before work. Often, I was able to see her in my mind's eye and check on her. In fact, I could actually tell which nurse had greeted her in the morning.

I remember saying to her as I walked in one day, 'Mum, who was the sexy male nurse who showered you this morning?'

She laughed, shaking her head and said, 'Trina do you ever bloody rest?!' She knew I had seen every little detail of her early morning schedule. But then she added, 'He was pretty nice looking though, Trine.' And we both burst into laughter.

One morning as I was getting ready to leave for the hospital, I received a call from the nurses saying I needed to get down there immediately. Mum had taken a turn for the worse. I called my brothers and told them what the nurses had said.

I was confused, as I hadn't had any indication she was that bad. I panicked and raced to the hospital thinking the worst. As I made my way to her room, I was stopped by one of her favourite nurses.

'Trine, she's not good. She's fading fast.'

I was so confused. Why wasn't I told by My People in spirit? I walked into her room and she looked very pale and lifeless. I came closer to her and stood over her chair. I was about to say my goodbyes. Immediately, she opened her eyes and smiled widely.

'Hello Trine, you're here early.'

I laughed with relief and said, 'Well, someone thought you weren't doing that well.'

'Really?' she said.

Two nurses came in and their faces said it all. They were completely dumbfounded. They smiled and asked if she wanted a cup of tea. I followed them out into the hallway and they both began to apologise.

'I'm so sorry, her breathing was nearly non-existent. She wasn't waking up. I don't know what happened.'

I assured them it was okay, and they were to call me any time they thought she wasn't doing well. But I knew this was a sign. I knew then that I had to become more organised and that she was leaving us soon.

I had kept up my exercise routine through all this, often going for a walk to the local football ground. It was quiet there and I liked the sense of nature. I was walking around the oval after I had done a few rounds of the grandstand stairs and it began to lightly rain. I appreciated the coolness of the raindrops falling on my skin.

But then I noticed something out of the corner of my eye. It was a kookaburra. He came closer to me, in fact so close I could almost touch him. He had something in his mouth, and I stopped.

I remembered the words from my guides: *When the bird who eats meat comes so close you can touch and the heavens open, it will be near.*

I stood in the rain, transfixed by the bird and the recognition of My People in spirit's words. The time was near for my mother to leave this earth. I allowed the raindrops and my tears to flow down my face as I thanked my guides for allowing me this knowledge. They knew it was important for me to get prepared for what was to come.

As a medium, we are often given information to help us prepare for the death of someone we will aid as they pass over to the other side. I have helped a number of people prepare for death and been at their side as they have taken their last breath. I am in what I call 'work-mode' as I do this, so I usually grieve before they pass. Then my focus is solely on the person I'm looking after. Then when they have died, I grieve again. Doing this kind of work is a privilege, but it is also hard and exhausting.

I spent many hours just talking with my mum, enjoying that special time. She would tell me stories of when she was young and what it was like to raise us kids. I talked of Dad and mentioned how I was disappointed I'd lost the only drawing he had done for me.

I said to her, 'I wonder if his brothers had any photographs or drawings. Maybe I should contact them.'

She immediately gave me a look and said, 'Don't you dare Trina, I don't want them to see me like this.' So, I agreed and promised I wouldn't.

A couple of weeks later I walked into her room and she gave me one of her looks. Mum would never ever hit us, not even a light smack. But she would give you this look that went right through you and her brown eyes would become deeper in colour.

'You're in trouble, Trina!'

I was shocked and confused. What was she talking about? I had no idea why I was in trouble. She went on to explain somehow my dad's brother had found out Mum was ill, and he had come to see her. I later saw him and as we sat having a coffee, he explained he had one of my father's paintings of three kittens he had painted when he was a young boy. He promised me he would send it to me as he thought it was important I have some of his artwork. He also had some photos of my paternal grandparents and he would send these as well.

Someone in spirit had been listening and knew it was my wish to have this little piece of my dad to physically touch and love. To this day, I still cherish this beautiful gift. I keep it safely packed amongst treasured items in my wooden trunk.

Over the next few weeks, I talked to Mum about what she wanted to happen as time drew near to her death. My younger brother had come to visit her, and she was talking quite openly about what her funeral should be like. Much to my dismay, she had decided her funeral must be in the Catholic church and it was to be a traditional funeral. This really surprised me as she hadn't been to church for many years. She wanted songs, and lots of them. But special songs, not necessarily hymns. Then my brother and I began to joke around a bit about what she should have as a song. We both tend to use our sense of humour at inappropriate times, which always ended with us both laughing when things were too serious, much to our mother's utter dismay.

But somewhere in that conversation, our mother had decided the didgeridoo should be playing. Then she laughingly added that maybe we could both do a traditional dance around her coffin.

We were all laughing at this, but then she stopped and said, 'I'm serious. I want the didgeridoo playing at my funeral.'

So, I nodded and agreed that this would be done.

Over the next week she became more and more fragile. I spent most of my time at her bedside, knowing her time to leave was nearing. She was now in a bed, only waking briefly and I was sleeping in the chair she had been nursed in throughout her illness. I was exhausted as I watched her sleep deeply, sometimes mumbling as she slipped deeper into a coma. All my guides were now with me and each time I got up to get water or go to the toilet, I could feel my Indian guide's headdress on my head.

I heard them say, 'We are with you Little One, we will not leave. The time is close.'

I was so darn tired, and the headdress felt heavy. I thanked them for their support and did mention it was getting too heavy for me to wear. Immediately it was lifted, but I could still feel them strongly by my side.

People came and went throughout the early evening and finally Mum and I were left in her room alone. I stroked her head and quietly spoke to her, thanking her for everything she had done for me growing up. I talked about Dad meeting her and how she must give him a kiss from me. And I watched as the lines on her face seemed to gently disappear. The hardship of life seemed to just gently fade from her face. The room was filled with people in spirit supporting her as her body weakened. Her breathing was laboured as I got back in my chair, but I thought she was settled. She wasn't ready to go. A calmness had entered her body and the room.

I closed my eyes, listening to her breathe. Then somehow, I dozed off for a minute.

I woke to her voice saying, 'Trine.'

I sat bolt upright thinking she was awake. Looking over, I saw her lifeforce leave her body and I knew she was leaving the earth plane.

I heard her say, 'I love you Trine, thank you.'

My beautiful mother was now dead.

The death of my mother hit me like a hammer smashing glass. She was my rock; someone I would talk to everyday. She was like a second mother to my children. But now she was gone and we were organising her funeral.

The funeral was indeed in the Catholic church as she had requested. The same church she was married in and each of her children were christened. The very church she had walked me past all those years ago when the magpies attacked me as a child.

We had discussed with the priest that our mother wanted special songs so there wouldn't be lots of hymns played, except for one that my mother's dear friend would play on the organ. My best friend would also recite a poem that was very dear to me. And instead of looking at only a coffin, we placed a beautiful photograph of my mother when she was younger on top of the coffin. We wanted everyone to see her beautiful smiling face. We were all there to celebrate her life, not a wooden box.

We had many songs that would describe my mother and how we felt about her. Some were chosen by each of us children. But we were struggling to find a song with a didgeridoo in it, as she had requested.

Out of the blue, my younger brother found a song by Rolf Harris called 'Sun Arise', which had a didgeridoo playing in the background. It was a beautiful song that was actually very fitting for our dear mum. Some of the words described her so well.

The song spoke of how each day as the sun rises it spreads light to the world, replacing darkness wherever it touched. Its energy giving light to whatever and whoever was in need. Our beautiful mother was a constant positive force in our lives. To us, she was a light like no other. The song summed up our mother perfectly. She was a beautiful shining light, just like the sunrise. Spreading her light wherever she went.

As her coffin was wheeled out of the church, we played this song loudly and I looked over at my brother and we smiled. The memory of her wanting us both to add a traditional dance around her coffin was strong in our minds. She certainly did spread light all around her wherever she went. I thought it was a beautiful way to say goodbye to a woman we loved dearly.

The funeral was finished, and her coffin was about to be placed in the ground by my brothers and her own brother. As they were placing her carefully in the ground, low and behold, one lone magpie swooped gracefully down, flying just inches above my older brother's head. He was startled and nearly dropped her, but just in the nick of time regained his composure. He looked over at me with a look of, *Did that really happen? Was that our mother?* I smiled and nodded. Yep, that was our mum making a bit of a statement. She was saying goodbye.

From that day forward, I knew magpies would always be with me wherever I went. Never again would I be afraid of them. Because in my mind, these birds I once saw as evil and to be feared, were a part of my mother's energy.

My guides in spirit have always said, those we love in spirit can connect with us in many wonderful ways. Legend says that birds are often messengers from Spirit, because they can fly up into the heavens but also land on Earth. They can take on the soul of those in spirit to deliver the message we need to know down here on Earth.

From that day on, magpies would become my family. My mother, my father, and in time, my older brother. They would show me family bonds and that love cannot be broken – no, not even by death.

In fact, I now have become somewhat like my mother with regard to magpies, but taken it even a little further. Wherever I go, three magpies will always appear. When I journeyed to Queensland to settle, I found they came even closer to me. They would appear at each house I lived at. Actually, they would often come into the house, making themselves quite at home.

I look forward to their visits and often they will bring their babies for me to feed and get to know. I never name the three adults, because they are my family in spirit. But each time they have new babies I name them according to their personality. They sit on my arm, as do my magpie family, and the young ones vie for my attention, often sitting on my head or pulling my hair gently to get my attention. The neighbours often shake their heads in disbelief as I sit at the front door with my magpies on my arms and legs, the older birds surrounding me as I play with their young. I'm sure they think I'm the crazy bird woman! But what they don't realise is these birds are my family and will always be so very important in my life.

My magpie family are never far from me or my thoughts. They often come to me when I need comfort or strength, or to relay knowledge I have missed. They sit listening to my joys, my troubles, my dreams of the future. I love this time with them, as it makes me feel peaceful and very much loved.

Each time they visit me I think of the family I have in spirit, still loving and supporting me as only a family can. But most of all, I think of my beautiful mum. No longer would I ever fear these birds, because I know my mother sent them to look after me. Who would have thought a magpie would be able to deliver such love and support? That a bird could signify such a beautiful bond that could never be broken, between mother and daughter, not even in death? My mother did, and I love her dearly for that.

* * * * * * * * * * *

A mother's love is special and reflects the unique bond that exists between a child and their mother. But we must remember a mother often expresses love to her children within the constraints of how she herself has experienced love. Hopefully, as she mothers her child and becomes more accustomed to the personality traits that child possesses, she adds her own unique blend of mothering.

Looking back at my own mother, I definitely see traits of my grandmother within her but also her own unique style of mothering. I also see in my own style of mothering, parts of my mother's influence on myself and again my own style of mothering. We must remember when we are blessed with a child, we are not hand delivered a roadmap on how to mother. Yes, there are definitely a lot of books on the subject, and of course these days good old Google to rely on as well. But even with all this information at our finger tips, motherhood is very much a trial and error experience. Basically, you learn as you go until we become more aware of the child's personality and their needs. Remember, we mothers are not perfect and we won't get everything right.

What lessons did my own mother teach me? Well, of course she taught me the basics most mothers will teach their daughters. How to cook, clean, sew and do the dreaded laundry. But what did she teach me at a soul level? Probably the strongest lesson she taught me would be how to keep going in the face of adversity. She taught me how to use my strength of will so that I could master anything challenging that was to come my way. I look at her strength and saw how she managed to battle on. But I also saw times when she really did need to stop and look after herself. That taught me it's important to sometimes ask for help or take a break so I don't become exhausted. Asking for help and looking after oneself is never being weak – it's absolutely necessary at times.

At a soul level, I think we learn a lot from our mothers.

A clairvoyant told me years ago, 'The women in your family have had a difficult journey. Remember you can change this, you don't have to follow their journey.'

And yes, I think my mother showed me through her own somewhat difficult life, that my life doesn't have to be filled with hardship. And that life is about making choices – based not only on what is good for others, but also making sure my choices were based on what I need as well. To be able to balance strength with fragility is a lesson I continue to try and learn to master.

This is just one of the many valuable lessons learned from my mother. I am sure if you take the time to observe your own mother, you will uncover many soul lessons she has taught you or is still teaching you to this day.

Chapter Three

MY BROTHER MY BLOOD

I know a man in spirit.
He is my brother, my blood.
He was a strong untamed character
Who often lived without limit.

He was born with different aspects of the mother and father.
Owning her stubbornness, strength and willingness to laugh.
His father's gifts of boxing and art.
A few drinks becoming a part of his life.
But really, he was unique, he was himself, he was like no other.

I hold memories of his wild days, the party and drinking days.
The times we laughed and shook our heads.
Thinking this young man would leave this world in a blaze.
Of times he would wake unable to recall the night before,
A grin on his face, his antics now just a haze.

But before long, he settled and became a father himself.
Each one his heart treasured.
Still unique and brash, but now more in tune with self.

Three beautiful children he nurtured and grew.
And through life's hardships and blessings,
He became someone new.

In my mind, still somewhat hard to tame.
He was always quick to react
And we never quite thought the same.

But he was my brother, my blood.
Our faces similar and neither liked to judge.
But each owned an opinion
That would not budge.
For there lies the stubbornness of our mother's blood.

Soon he was to battle an unbeatable fight.
Strong body beginning to weaken and wither.
But still his spirit held strong.
His mind and heart clasping to life so tight.

There would be no talk of funerals and death.
No, his mind would not give in,
Not even when his body began to struggle to gain breath.

Each child so close to him,
Loving and supporting him as he travelled this painful journey.
Each one like their father, possessing all of his traits within.

The body began to tire, and death came like a flood.
A look of surprise, a look of love.
One solitary tear rolling gently down the cheek
Of my brother, my blood.

The time had come to leave this world.
But each time I look at his children,
I see and hear my brother, my blood.
The world they had known now hurled.

We know he would stay if he could.
His children's mind and hearts hold a gift within.
The memory of one man,
No other can replace and no one would.

He was my brother, my blood.
He was more than his boxing and art.
To us he was a man like no other.
For this man in spirit would always be our blood.

I said at the start of this book that it is my belief that all those we come into contact with, will teach us at some level, or we will teach them. Some of these lessons will scratch the surface and others will be forever etched on your soul.

All sorts of people come and go throughout our lives, each one leaving a mark that can be either positive or negative. A mark symbolising hardship or joy. We all experience both at some time throughout our lives.

Your family are significant teachers in life and hold the promise of many soul lessons, if you take the time to see them. Of course, we are human beings filled with emotions, opinions and patterns. Some of these, we have made ourselves. And at other times, those around us have helped create these emotions, opinions, and patterns, whether good or bad.

My older brother Peter was quite a character. Like anyone who has a sibling relationship, we all know that at times we will have differing opinions. We can have different ways of seeing the world, even if we grew up under the same roof. But when it comes down to it, most of us will agree that the old saying of 'blood is thicker than water' often rings true.

I often found my brother difficult to understand as we were growing up. We were just so different in so many ways. But of course, I also loved him dearly. Even though at times I sometimes wondered how on Earth we could be related as we were so very different when it came to our attitudes and outlook on life. But if I'm honest, we also shared many similarities, as siblings often do. Why wouldn't we? We are related by blood.

He was loud and brash; I was shy and reserved.

He could be hot-headed; I was very placid.

He was spontaneous and didn't think about his actions; I thought about every little detail before making a move.

He was an artist; I couldn't draw a stick figure.

But –

He was creative and so was I.

He was stubborn and so was I.

He was opinionated and so was I.

He would stand his ground and so would I.

He was loyal and kind to those he loved. And so was I.

One of the greatest lessons this man taught me was to stand in my own power. To do this, I took a very different path to my brother. He was a boxer and spoke his mind often, not really knowing when to be quiet. And if he had had a few drinks under his belt he could become quite aggressive.

But one thing I can say, is that my brother was always unashamedly himself. No, he wasn't perfect. But who is?

For many years, I grew up under the shadow of my older brother. As a young child, I was often seen by my mother as the 'good' one, the responsible one. And because of this, I often took on the role of keeping things in line while Mum was at work.

But as I aged and began to socialise, I soon found out everyone expected me to be like my brother. Full of bravado and someone who lived on the edge. Well, did they get a shock! I may have looked like him, but our personalities were indeed very different. I was quiet, in fact very shy, and most times made sure I wasn't getting into too much trouble.

My brother was a well-built man, but only small in stature like our mum and dad. So, when he was younger, he was given the nickname 'Titch' by his friends. As his sister, I refused point blank to call him Titch, he was always Pete to me. I'm not sure if my name was hard to remember or people just wanted to associate me with him, but often I would be called Little Titch by his friends. To be honest, I detested this because for one, I had my own name, and two, I didn't want to be seen as reckless as him. I just wanted to be me!

Like my father, Peter had the most wonderful gift for drawing. His artwork was something that everyone, including myself, thought was brilliant. He could draw anything, and the image would just seem to jump off the page and speak to you. Like our father in his younger days, he would drink to excess. But, unlike our father, his moods could change quite dramatically. He could change from happy-go-lucky and giving, to fearless, argumentative and aggressive.

Even though he was my elder brother, it was usually me looking out for him rather than him playing the protective brother. One Sunday afternoon I was coming back from visiting with one of my friends and as I was walking past the local park, I was drawn to a person laying in the sun.

I noticed he was extremely sunburnt and as I focused on him, My People in spirit came close and whispered in my ear, 'Little One, it's the brother.'

I walked over and he was sprawled out on his back. Hawaiian shirt open and sunglasses still placed on his eyes. He was red raw, and I knew he would be feeling extremely sorry for himself if I didn't wake him or at least move him to the shade. Well, I tried to wake him, but he was out to it and from the smell I could tell he had had a very big night! So, I grabbed his arm and dragged him under a tree so he wouldn't get burnt any further.

He arrived home some hours later looking very red and very dehydrated and as any younger sister would, I laughed at him! But then I explained I had actually moved him to the shade when I realised I couldn't wake him.

He looked at me and thanked me, shaking his head saying, 'It was a big night.'

There were times when he was out of control, that I could sometimes talk him round. And at other times I knew I just had to let him go on his destructive path and hope he didn't do too much damage to himself or others.

But as time moved on, he became a father and all those reckless days seemed to fade. His main focus was then placed on his three children who he adored with all his heart. Unfortunately, at this time he had also chosen to step away from our family for quite a few years for reasons that he could only deal with. This caused great distress to my mother, yet not once did she speak of him badly.

By the time he reunited with our family I had grown into myself. I was now a little more outspoken and knew where I needed to focus. And even though we were still very different in temperament, we became a little closer. As a young girl, I found it difficult to stand up to my brother or deal with his confrontational attitude. But now that I had grown into a young woman, I saw the need to be me! I remember his look of surprise the first time I spoke up for myself and didn't agree with his opinion.

He smiled and said, 'Oh, who's a stubborn little girl now?'

I knew he wasn't saying this with malice, he was proud I had learned to say what was on my mind. He knew we had both changed. Time and life experiences will do that, hey?

He had taken his artwork further and began to carve the most extraordinary pictures on emu eggs. He also began working as a tattooist, which he became very well known for in our community.

He would often say to me, 'Trine, we need to tattoo the Harrington Coat of Arms on you, so everyone knows you're a Harrington!'

I'd reply, 'Pete, I know I'm a Harrington and that's all that matters. And anyway, I have no intentions of marking this beautiful body of mine.'

While Pete was away from the family, he had contracted Q fever from his work in the abattoirs and his immune system never seemed to fully recover. As our mother became sicker, he also showed signs something wasn't right with his body.

One day I was having a coffee with him at his house and he asked if I thought something major was wrong with him. I began to ask my guides and all of a sudden, I became overpowered with the smell of hospitals. So much so, I thought I was going to throw up. I didn't seem to be able to come out of what I was feeling and everything around me was moving and reeling. I felt out of control and overwhelmed. I quickly made an excuse and took my leave. But as I sat in my car recovering, I knew something was drastically wrong. I knew my brother, my blood, was very ill, and a great sadness came over me.

As time went on, his body became weaker and the weight began to fall away from his once muscular body. He found it difficult to eat and eventually was diagnosed with cancer of the esophagus, a cancer usually only present in the elderly. He was forty-five years old.

But as his illness progressed, I saw the Peter I always loved come forward. His caring open heart, that sense of humour and dry wit. His sense of courage and that attitude of 'I can do anything' was so strong. He began to listen to some of my advice – not all of it, mind you. But most of what I suggested he took on board.

Each time I saw him if I didn't lean over to give him a kiss he would say, 'Where's my kiss? You're my sister, we're family. Don't ever forget that.'

And I'd smile because I knew we were closer now than we ever had been.

Cancer of the esophagus is a very cruel disease. By then I'd cared for a lot of people with illness, but my brother's illness began to rattle my beliefs. I remember visiting him one day and disposing of the bloody mess he had to keep spitting out of his mouth. He told me to stop, let it be and just sit with him. So, I did and we talked.

Leaving his hospital ward, I was SO angry! I said to my guides, 'This isn't fair! If he was an animal, we would shoot him! He's going through too much! Let him die! This isn't right! It just isn't fair!'

I was distraught and all I could smell was his illness, it invaded my senses. I actually wanted my brother to die, because I loved him and didn't want him to go through any more pain.

A few days later I was at his bedside, knowing he was soon to leave this world for the next. He was now in a coma. His wife told me that during the night in his restless sleep he kept saying, 'So many lessons to learn, so many lessons.'

I knew the time was near for him to go.

He opened his eyes in surprise and looked at me searchingly as if to say, *What's going on?*

I leaned forward and smiled and told him gently 'It's time Pete, it's okay.'

Then I stepped away so his wife and boys could come close and be with him. We watched as a single tear slowly ran down his cheek and I knew without a doubt it was a sign he didn't want to leave his beloved children and his wife. Peter took his last breath that evening, his two sons and wife at his side. His daughter arrived just after his spirit left his body. His time of struggle was now over, he was free from pain. He was now in the loving arms of our father and mother.

In our family, great importance is placed on the songs played at the funeral of our loved ones. 'Eye of the Tiger,' the theme from the boxing movie *Rocky* was the first song played before I was to say his eulogy. I think it was the most fitting song for my brother. He showed such courage in his fight against this horrible illness.

We only disagreed once in his time of dealing with his illness. A doctor had told him he didn't know how long he had to live. It could be a month or five years, he just didn't know.

Peter, being Peter, immediately said, 'It will be five years then. I'll fight this with whatever I have.'

And when he told me this I looked away, he noticed this and got annoyed with me.

'You don't think I can do you? You don't think I can last that long, do you?'

I looked at him and said, 'I hope you stay as long as you can, Pete.'

Defiantly, he said, 'Watch me!'

I knew he couldn't last five years, and I wanted him to get his family ready for his death. But he wouldn't have a bar of it. So, we never spoke of his approaching death again.

As 'Eye of the Tiger' played, I felt his energy near me. And low and behold, one single magpie came close to the podium I rested my eulogy on. It began to sing so strongly, watching me intently. My mother in spirit was showing me she was there to give me strength.

I started my eulogy with saying, 'Peter would hate it if I portrayed him as an angel because we all know he wasn't.'

Everyone immediately chuckled and nodded their heads in agreement. I was honoured to be by his side as he passed, and equally honoured to write and deliver his eulogy. He was a great teacher in my life. My brother, my blood.

A few weeks after his death, a song was continually playing through my head. It became so strong it was starting to annoy me. Peter's wife came to visit, and I mentioned how annoyed I was with this song and it must belong to someone in spirit.

She asked the name of the song and I told her: 'Whatever Will Be, Will Be' by Doris Day.

She began laughing, which annoyed me even more. Then she told me, 'Trine, it's your brother's favourite song.'

A string of profanities came from my mouth because I just didn't think he would even like that type of song. But now I knew he was connecting with me and he had brought that song forward so I would know it was definitely him.

Peter will often mess with the fire detectors in my house and when his wife would visit he would always set them off, creating a huge noise!

I'd say, 'Ok, ok, we know you're here now Pete!' and laugh.

Even in spirit he had to make a statement – a loud statement! But hey, that's my brother to a tee!

My brother taught me it's not necessary to be aggressive or confrontational. People don't need to be apprehensive of you, in order for you to own your own power and stand up for yourself. When you own who you truly are, warts and all, that's when you truly own your own power! That's when you can do anything you put your mind to without fear of being shunned or judged. He taught me that you must believe in yourself enough to create strong and healthy boundaries with people in your life.

I have had the privilege of watching his boys grow to become men and fathers themselves. Each one has struggled at some point to cope with life, but they have inherited their dad's courage and his 'I can do anything' attitude shine through them. I know my brother is so proud of the wonderful men and fathers they have both become. I know he stands with each of his three children, guiding them from spirit the best way he can. I have no doubt that he will always be their guiding light throughout their lives.

A few months after my brother died, he came to me in my dreams. With a big grin on his face he said, 'TRINE, you were right. We do go on!'

I knew exactly what he meant and smiled. Peter often had doubts there was a life after death. Don't get me wrong, he always talked of Dad and Mum in spirit being around him. But I often saw a little bit of doubt or questioning creeping into his mind. Or maybe he was just a little worried he was going downstairs and not upstairs in spirit. Seriously I can't imagine my brother sitting on a cloud playing a harp, that's for sure!

Perhaps somewhere along that journey of being siblings, I taught my brother, my blood, a lesson too. And now I have three beautiful magpies supporting and guiding me from spirit: my father, mother and brother.

Chapter Four

PHOTOGRAPHS AND MEMORIES

An elder who seemed to me to have the wisdom of centuries,
Poring over photographs and memories.

Pale skin, soulful eyes, and fragile walk.
A child listening to her talk.

Sitting next to her fire,
An elder I so admire.

A daughter, a wife, a woman who gave birth.
An elder, my grandmother who walked this earth.

Fruit cake, bread and butter pudding, and rhubarb she would bake.
As a child I would often wish she would bake a sweet sponge cake.

Her barley soup stirred on top of her stove
My taste buds thought it was a treasure trove.

She spoke of people long gone to Spirit,
Of how these loved ones learned their limit.

Days gone by filled with hardship and fun,
Knowing when to acknowledge the day is now done.

Long ago I learned to listen and heed my grandmother.
She was my only, I had no other.

Grandmother now in spirit, a hand on my shoulder,
standing at my side
Helping all those who come to me find their stride.

Growing up, I didn't have a great deal to do with my grandparents. My paternal grandparents died at a young age, and my maternal grandfather also died reasonably young. So, I really only had a connection with my maternal grandmother.

I think grandparents are so very important. To me, they are the keepers of stories. If you take the time to listen to their stories, they tell us of a very different time. They can teach us so many things. They hold a wisdom that, I think, is sometimes disregarded these days.

My advice is, if you are lucky enough to have grandparents still alive, then spend as much time as you can with them. You will learn so much from these wonderful souls.

My own grandmother was named Eva and she was a very strong, stoic woman. She wasn't a grandmother that gathered you up within her arms or told you she loved you that often. When she was younger, she contracted polio and was extremely ill and because of this, limped due to one of her legs being weaker than the other. She never really talked about her illness but I'm sure it would have been a very difficult thing to deal with as a child.

My earliest memories of my grandmother were when my mother, brothers and I came to live with her, while my dad was away hay carting to earn money for the family. Her house was a big, sprawling old home with intricate metal ceilings, and an outside laundry and toilet.

When people came to visit, they would all end up in the kitchen chatting away over a cup of tea. I was always amazed by the fact the women in my family would announce, 'I'll put the kettle on' whenever there was a problem to deal with. As a child, I would often think this kettle must be an amazing thing if it can solve all their problems. But as I grew older, I soon understood it was merely a ritual to lead them into trying to discuss how to tackle the problem.

I loved the large back yard and wide verandahs that surrounded the house. I spent many hours out back with my dog Lassie, just laying my head on her tummy while drinking my bottle. I had a bottle until I was four, nearly five. It was my comfort thing when I felt overwhelmed. I would just lay on my dog, leg over one knee, sucking on my bottle, moving my elevated leg to a rhythm that only I could hear.

I also remember the joy of eating pomegranates in my grandmother's yard. It's a fruit we don't see too often these days. I loved how when you opened the pomegranate, you would discover a beautiful pattern of brilliant red seeds inside. I would spend many moments just sitting in the sun, slowly taking each seed into my mouth and discovering the unusual sweet and tart sensation as it flowed onto my taste buds. Still to this day, I find a calmness to eating this fruit, just as I did when I was a child.

In this house I understood it was important to be quiet, as Gran really didn't like noise at all. Poor Mum would constantly be telling us not to wake Gran up from her afternoon sleeps. There were also many times when I felt Gran wasn't that impressed with my father, which I guess was understandable. Every mother is protective of her children, and she saw her daughter often struggle due to my father's drinking.

Gran was a very superstitious woman and at times I found some of her superstitions to be confusing. She never allowed wattle or peacock feathers in the house, among other things. In fact, I distinctly remember my older brother giving her a set of porcelain elephants and when she opened his present and saw one of the elephant's trunks was pointing down, she immediately smashed it on the floor. My brother was horrified and confused, the look on his face said it all! She scooped him up and apologised, explaining it was bad luck to have it in her house. She always had these different sayings, and I sometimes find myself using them in a reading.

One of her favourite sayings was, 'I must have run over a China man in my last life.' Which meant she was going through a tough time. Another was, 'There's always more than one way to skin a cat.' As a child I was horrified to even think she would contemplate hurting a cat. But it was just her way of saying we can do things in many different ways.

Eventually, we moved out to a commission house. Gran also moved to a smaller house, as age began to catch up with her. So, I only spent time with her when my mother would visit and take us with her.

As I began to mature, I spent more time with my gran, sometimes even staying with her overnight while the boys and my uncles went off and did boy things! I loved these times. I would sit and listen to her talk about how she grew up. Times when she travelled on horse and cart. Of the dunny man who came to collect the sanitary pans from the outside toilets. Of China men with long plaited pigtails. I loved getting to know her better and understood her life had been very hard and that's why she could sometimes be a bit aloof.

She also spoke of her own mother, who was referred to by all as 'Mother' and how she would see dead people and had prophecy dreams. I would lay in a single bed in her bedroom listening to her talk about this woman I never knew, and I'd think, *I'm like this woman*. Even though I had never met her when she was alive, she just seemed to resonate with me. There were many times when I felt her energy or heard the words 'It's okay, Mother is here.' But it wasn't until I was a little older that I found out who was actually saying these words of comfort to me from Spirit.

My gran had softened in her age and we spent a lot of time poring over old photographs she had in a cardboard box in her bedroom cupboard. She would haul this box out and we would sit on the floor, Gran telling me stories as we looked through the many black and white photographs.

At different times she would hand me a photograph and ask, 'What do you think of this one, Trine?'

I'd look at the picture and things would start to pop into my mind or vision. I would start to tell her a 'story' about the photograph and she would listen and smile. I know now that she was helping me discover my abilities, one of them being reading photographs.

My gran died at the age of seventy-two from cancer of the larynx. As her illness progressed, she had lost her ability to eat and survived purely on frozen milk. She also lost her ability to use her voice and only spoke in a whisper. She died not long after my father on 11 December and again Christmas became a time to remember.

Gran now stands with me in each reading I do, overseeing how I work. She makes sure I don't say anything inappropriate, like 'profanities' as she calls them. Often, I run things by her when a person in spirit uses words I'm not allowed to use, and she gives me an alternative for that word that she finds more suitable.

She is not classed as a guide though. She is my grandmother, a loved one in spirit that wants to aid and support me in my work. I find it somewhat funny, as I often thought as a child that she was a little apprehensive of the world of spirit. I think that was because her own mother would tell her in detail what she saw clairvoyantly. Mother saw people in spirit the way they actually died. I remember Gran telling me her own mother saw a woman hanging by her neck from her clothesline one day and it had shaken her.

Mother didn't always have control of how Spirit showed themselves to her, which can be quite a problem. I think it would be very difficult to see the graphic details of a death and not be able to stop those images. I would imagine it must've been extremely hard for her to maintain some semblance of a normal life. I learned from that and made my own rules with regards to how Spirit comes to me, but it did take some years to work out how to do this.

Until I worked out how to gain control, I was often startled by the dead. Imagine going into your bedroom and seeing someone sitting on your bed and you have no idea who they are! Or, imagine getting out of bed to go to the toilet and then turning around to see a man you don't know standing in the hallway when you returned! It would often take me a few seconds to realise the people were actually dead and just wanted to talk to me. Often, the fight or flight reflexes kick in and your first instinct is to run, thinking a living person was invading your space. But I can tell you, there were a number of occasions in my teenage years when I would get a fright and a number of well-chosen swear words would leave my mouth. But that's okay, Gran wasn't in ear shot to hear them and I'd usually end up giggling at myself for not realising they were people from Spirit.

Yes, I know, you are all thinking I'd be more frightened knowing he was dead, but seriously I've never really been frightened of dead people. They have always been a constant in my life.

I remember when I lived in Gran's house, spending time with an elderly man in spirit. He was often in my room during the day and played the violin beautifully. And seriously, to this day I don't know who this man was. But as a little girl, I thought he was wonderful and very entertaining.

Most times, living people are more of a problem to me than any dead person I've come across. Dead people just come to you as they are, no masks, no facades. Whereas with living people, I found you had to really read their emotions and agendas to know them completely and whether they were trustworthy.

I grew to know my grandmother better as we both grew with age. I knew she loved me and could only show that love in her own particular way.

While she has been in spirit I have grown to love her deeply and understand her more fully. I feel her strength standing by me each day and I know she loves to work with me as I do my readings. No, I don't get a lot of jokes or laughter coming from her, that hasn't changed! In fact, I often show her different Friday Funny Memes that I like to put on my Facebook site, only to be told they are definitely not appropriate! So those ones go to a dear friend of mine which causes us both a great deal of laughter and then I pick one my gran has deemed funny but appropriate. No, she hasn't got a great sense of mischievous humour but she brings in something more important – a feeling of strength and respect that allows me to represent Spirit in the way they should be represented.

When I think of my grandmother I think of stories. She was a woman that always had a story to tell. As a child I understood there were some stories she found too painful to talk about. I have since been privy to those stories over the time she has been in spirit and understand why she kept those to herself.

In some way, my grandmother taught me to speak of my own stories. Your stories give others insight into who you are and they then can understand you more fully. Also, through sharing your stories, the people listening may also look more fully into their own journey. For this, I'm blessed to have had her in my life. I feel blessed to be able to say I'm her granddaughter.

My grandmother has taught me so much, especially since moving into the world of spirit. As a child I watched her hold her head high and be strong when life was hard. I intuitively knew she had so much wisdom to pass on to me as I was growing up. She showed me it was okay to explore the world of spirit. But she also made sure I also understood that not everyone would appreciate the fact Spirit existed and I was privy to their world. She did this through storytelling and letting me know about the life her own mother lived.

My grandmother also taught me it is extremely important to be of service to self – first, before you can fully be of service to others. There is an old saying that reminds me of my grandmother perfectly, and explains the act of being of service to self: *You cannot pour from an empty cup*. It is so true, but we often forget these words as we go about our busy lives. It is another lesson to be learned by us all here on Earth.

To do this work, there is a need for detachment and strength. Otherwise, you can become overwhelmed by all you hear, see and feel. But there is also a need to be empathetic to others and to self. We also need to understand when working with Spirit that we are their voice, and must always work in a respectful and ethical way.

My grandmother taught me all these things and to this day continues to teach me each time I read for each client that comes to me for guidance.

Chapter Five

A Gift Like No Other

Some people say I have been given a gift at birth,
And yes, my senses show me things like no other.
I see beautiful things that are not from this earth.

It has taken time to discover the many facets of my gift.
At times struggling to come to terms with this way of living.
Times where all I could manage to do in my life was drift.

But throughout my years I have had something for
which I am forever grateful.
My People in spirit standing by my side.
No matter the circumstances, I knew they were there and faithful.

Their words of encouragement and love guiding me through life.
Never once leaving me to fight my battles alone.
Teaching me all they can about their world of spirit, the afterlife.

They are My People in spirit, those I have always called my family.
Their love and wisdom helping me to stand tall and be who I am.
Teaching me with love the wonders of life, death and alchemy.

To me, My People are the true gift I have been given.
A gift no one on this earth can take away.
A love that a soul gives to another from heaven.

Pure unconditional love, soul love
That makes my life better and I feel so blessed
To have been guided by My People in spirit sent from above.

I know without a doubt we live on after death.
Yes, I see, hear and feel those in spirit. I am in a life of service.
But, the gift like no other is My People.
I will love them until my last breath.

Since I can remember, I have had my beautiful guides in spirit by my side, walking with me through each and every step of my journey. As I aged, they became an integral part of my life. So much so, that for many years I have seen them as my beloved family.

I've had many spirit guides come and go over my lifetime, each one teaching me something valuable, then quietly stepping back. Sometimes they return when I need to remember or take action on their lessons.

Everyone has at least one guide that stands by them throughout their journey. Some people will know intuitively they are there. Some will have daily interactions with them and others will have no idea at all about their presence

What is a spirit guide? The best way I can explain it is to say they are people who have walked the earth many times, in many incarnations. As they experienced these lives they have learned the lessons of the soul. They have then chosen to help the living learn the lessons given to them by the soul, by guiding them from spirit in this lifetime. Having learned the many lessons of the soul, there is no need to return to future incarnations. These souls will now offer their wisdom and advice to those who are still to learn their soul lessons here on Earth.

I don't like to say I have favourite guides, because each and every one has taught me something valuable and touched my heart deeply. But, there are two guides who have been my constant companions. They have encouraged and loved me through the many ups and downs of my life.

My Blue Dog Indian

When I was a young child, I had what I thought was a blue dog visit me on a number of occasions. Often this would happen when I was a little fearful of all that was going on in my bedroom at night. As any child can be, I was sometimes a little nervous of all the sounds the night brings when you are tucked up in bed trying to sleep. And unlike children these days, we weren't often brought into the beds of our parents or even had a night light of any kind.

I also had to contend with the many different spirit people who would come and go. None were scary or negative, but I was a child and I did not know these people. So, at times I did feel a little overwhelmed and even a bit apprehensive.

My Blue Dog would appear at the end of my bed. To me he was the most beautiful dog I had ever seen. He seemed to glow with a blue shimmer. An aura of blue surrounded him as he came closer to me and laid his head on my bed. I loved his visits; he brought such a feeling of strength and calmness. With my hand on My Blue Dog's head I soon drifted off into a peaceful slumber. When I woke in the morning he was always gone.

The years passed and one night I was laying in my bed feeling a bit lost and unable to sleep. I began to see the shimmer of blue light I always saw when My Blue Dog came to visit me. I began to concentrate on this light waiting for him to appear and soon he was there just watching me. I motioned for him to come, but he stayed still. I was confused. Why wasn't he coming close?

Then My Blue Dog seemed to gently fade, and a Native American Indian was standing in his place with the most beautiful smile. He seemed so big and strong, yet I could feel his gentle energy surround me and I began to smile. Somehow, I knew this man was My Blue Dog.

'Little One, I didn't want you to be frightened of me, so I came as the dog for a number of years so you could become accustomed to my energy. You have seen my form before, but the memory is lost. One day we will revisit this.'

My Navajo Indian stayed with me for many years. We would spend hours talking about his life on Earth and the things I needed to experience and accomplish. He was a huge man, yet I never ever felt threatened or worried by his presence. He taught me to have patience with myself when I found things to be difficult. He would sit with me when I was overwhelmed and lost. He helped me to come to terms with the loss of my dad and encouraged me to grieve when I needed to. He showed me how his tribe would use the land and what was necessary to eat and drink to keep my body healthy. He stood with me when I did my readings and showed me how to clairvoyantly see more clearly. He made me rest when I thought I needed to do more. But most of all, I knew without a doubt he loved me at a soul level, and I could trust him with my life.

One day in meditation he came to me, saying it was nearly time for him to step back from me and that he had taught me all he could. I was shocked and completely devastated.

'No, you can't. I can't do this without you.'

I was sobbing and couldn't imagine my life without him. At this time in my life I had been at the bedside of several of my loved ones as they took their last breath. I felt like everyone was leaving me. I just could not cope with the knowledge My Indian, as I call him, was also leaving. I began to get angry.

'Why? Why do you have to go? I'm doing all you asked, why do you have to leave? It's not fair!' I turned to Claire, a guide I'd had with me even before My Indian had appeared. 'Why, Claire? Why does he have to go?'

She smiled and touched my shoulder. 'It is time, Little One. He will return from time to time. But now he must step away.'

I was distraught, and tears were streaming down my face. 'This isn't fair, it's not fair! Everyone I love is leaving me and I'm supposed to just keep helping people find their way. What do I do? What do I get from all this?'

Both My Indian and Claire just smiled and sat there. By this time, the anger had boiled up inside me and I was so overwhelmed with emotion.

I stood up and said, 'Okay, right! If he's going and I have to keep doing this without him, then you have to promise me you will never leave me, Claire.' I looked at her with such defiance, waiting for her to answer.

She smiled and waited for what seemed to be an eternity to me and said, 'I will never leave you, Little One. I will do as you have asked and be with you until you take your last breath. I have always been with you, Little One. This will not change.'

My body softened and I was somewhat surprised at my outburst. I had never raised my voice to my guides, my beautiful teachers, and now I was ashamed of my behaviour.

'I'm sorry, I didn't mean to get upset. I just can't bear to lose another person I love. I'm sorry I yelled at you both.'

Both Claire and My Indian smiled and I felt their love surround me. My Indian came close and touched my cheek gently.

'Remember, Little One, I am but a breath away. You will see me again. Do not fear, always remember your blue dog will watch over you, even from afar.'

Then, his image began to fade into the blue dog until finally just the shimmer of blue could be seen. Then there was nothing.

Claire was at my side as I sobbed. It was as if I could feel my own heart breaking. It hurt. I was exhausted.

'It is good to grieve a love that has been so strong and now lost, Little One. Feel the grief. You have been through many things with the soul you call My Indian. But as you grieve, remember you are loved beyond this world.'

I lay down, Claire by my side and allowed the tears to continue to flow. My Indian was gone.

For many months I grieved the loss of My Indian, until finally my heart began to heal. But my heart never forgot the memory of an Indian man who was my teacher, my guide, my protector and my dear friend.

At different times throughout my life, My Indian has indeed returned as he promised, to check on this Little One. But he never stays for very long. I now know it was necessary for my growth for him to step back when he did.

Many years later on what I had dubbed The Pomegranate Retreat, I was actually shown the moment I truly first saw My Indian in his full body as he come to me as a child.

Whenever I go on retreat it is always a very intense time of self-evaluation and working with my guides. I had been warned this retreat would be very harrowing, but also necessary for my growth and healing.

My alchemy guide came to me in meditation and said, 'Little One, tell me the times you remember your mother held you?'

I thought for a while and answered, 'The day I left for Queensland and at the wake of my father's funeral.'

He looked in my eyes and said firmly, 'This is not true. She held you many, many times.'

I looked at him, feeling confused. I seriously could not remember her holding me, even though I knew she loved me dearly.

'We must take you back in time, to when you were very young. You have disassociated at this time and this is why you cannot remember a great deal, apart from those interactions you had with those in spirit.'

I felt very apprehensive about doing this. He was right – I could only remember small snippets of my time staying in my grandmother's house. I remembered the times I interacted with those in spirit, but couldn't recall playing with my mother or her holding me. I couldn't even remember her putting me to bed each night!

He patted my arm and smiled to reassure me I would be okay.

I felt myself slip deeply into meditation and saw I was in my grandmother's house at the age of four. I was in a darkened room, confused as I didn't know what was happening to me. I couldn't escape. There was no way out of the room and I felt helpless and scared. I couldn't breathe. My body was being used in a way I couldn't understand and I was frightened.

Then everything seemed to go black, and immediately I saw a blue haze in front of me. Everything else seemed to disappear. I saw the face of an Indian and all I could feel was complete love and compassion. He looked into my eyes and held my face gently in his hands.

He said, 'Little One, look at me. Look only at me and feel the love I have for you. Let go of everything else and be with me in this moment. Just you and I together.'

I did as he said. I knew in that moment he was there to protect me. I found it easier to breathe now. The room disappeared. All that was happening disappeared. I felt safe. I felt protected. I felt loved. My Indian was with me.

Time seemed to disappear. Before long, I was out of the dark room and my mother was calling me. She could see something was wrong and asked if I was okay.

All I could manage to say to her was, 'My tummy hurts.'

She pulled me into her arms and sat with me on her knee for a long time, just cuddling me and stroking my hair.

I came out of the meditation and My Indian was standing with the alchemy guide. Both were smiling and their eyes were filled with concern and love.

'We had to take you back to that time, Little One, because with our help, you had distanced yourself and your mind from all that happened in that room. And in doing this, your mind also distanced itself from the loving memories and events that occurred too. This is why you never remembered your mother cradling you. This is why you have no memory of her physical love and the soft words only a mother gives a child. We had to step forward to save you from the hurt you would suffer through no fault of your own, even though you knew we were there and you interacted with us on a daily basis. This was the moment we all became a constant in your life and were never to leave your side.'

I sat back, somewhat dazed. Memories of my mother flooded into my mind. Times she played with me and we laughed. Times she hugged me and nurtured her little girl. All those beautiful moments any child should treasure and remember seemed to flow back into my mind.

'Your mother loved you dearly, Little One, and you knew that. But due to events that occurred that day, your mind distanced from all the physical nurturing she had given you as you grew.'

I allowed myself to go over the events they had shown me and realised I had completely removed that day and its events from my mind. I had remembered other, different incidents that took place in my grandmother's house. But until that day on retreat, I had no recollection of what had transpired on that one particular day, or how my beautiful Indian had come to my rescue.

No wonder I felt such grief for this beautiful man when he had to step away from me all those years later in my life.

Claire

As I mentioned earlier, Claire had been with me even before My Indian. She often comes to me dressed in a long cape. She has a witty, dry sense of humour and such a caring nature. I can't actually recall when I haven't had Claire around me, although her presence became so much stronger when as a young woman I went into spiritual development. It was a process where I had to learn to hone my abilities stronger and more professionally.

Claire has been a constant in my life. She sits with me in each reading, helping me to fine tune all the details I receive from those coming to me in spirit. She also sits with me when I am teaching meditation and is always a source of entertainment and knowledge to myself and my students. But Claire is more than just the things she helps me with regarding my abilities. She is my much-loved companion and dearest friend.

The first silent retreat I went on, which Claire had encouraged me to do, she showed me a life where we were sisters and I could feel the bond of love between us so very strongly. As I sat in the retreat house, the walls began to fade and everything disappeared. I closed my eyes, knowing I was about to receive information from my guides. I was moving into that state where the world of the living disappears and I'm totally in the world of spirit. A world where I always feel safe and loved.

I saw us as we walked along a road. It was cold and I was only young. Claire was not much older than myself, but she felt like she was my mother looking after my wellbeing. As I watched the past life, she stopped on the side of a dirt road and showed me a tattered bag and all the special things inside it – stones and crystals and little essential things. I could feel her love and the fact she took full responsibility for my wellbeing without a thought for her own. I sat in this state for an hour, just watching what she showed me through my mind. I knew without a doubt that in that life, she loved me dearly. And now, in this life too, as she guides me from the world of spirit.

Many years later I had a very strong urge to go into retreat. It became stronger and stronger, until I made a date and found a place I felt comfortable going to for my retreat. When I go on retreat, the place must be surrounded by nature and have places to walk. It must feel secure and safe to me. There is no talking or interacting with others, no social media, television or radio is allowed and only food that can help the body. So, you guessed it, no potato chips, my favourite treat, come on retreat with me.

Walking into the retreat I had chosen, I began to explore all it had to offer. I was impressed. The energy was light, it felt safe and comforting, and it was beautiful and quiet. The only sounds were the birds and a few distant voices from rural properties surrounding the house. The garden was beautiful, with towering trees leading into a forest. I even discovered a little wooden bridge that led into the bush. It immediately made me think of my journey and what would transpire on this silent retreat.

After a couple of days working with my guides and taking the most wonderful long walks, I sat down to meditate. I began to see my ancestors, including my father telling me to write my story. My mother had come to me the night before. So many people filled the room. I saw people that don't usually come to me often, like my aunts and my paternal grandmother, who told me she also loved to dance and that my father never got over her death. So many of my ancestors surrounded me and sent me love. I sat in the room fully focused on all I was shown.

My guides then came forward, showing me they and my family stand with me in all I do. Claire talked of our past life together, how she loved to make me laugh and would often make up stories so I wouldn't be afraid when things were hard. She showed herself putting on different personas, trying to draw my attention to her, rather than all the hard things we were going through.

At one stage as a young child, my boot had come apart. My thick stocking had a hole in it and my foot was becoming cold and sore. Claire took her shoe off and I wore hers, which was way too big, but she had no shoe at all. She began to hobble like an old lady, her voice now sounding like she had the years of an elderly lady.

'Come, Little One, we have to find the treasure – we must look for the treasure.'

I looked up at her wide-eyed. 'Treasure? What would be the treasure?'

Claire smiled. She could see I was beginning to forget about my foot. She was bent over, pretending to walk with a stick as she continued to talk.

'Oh, my Little One, there will be many things. Warm soup with meat in it, beautiful dresses and warm coats.'

I stopped walking. 'Will there be boots?' I asked.

She stopped and held my face between her hands. 'Yes, Little One, there will be fancy boots of all colours. Some with buttons and others you will tie.' She pulled my hand and we continued to walk; in fact, I began to skip, not thinking of my large boot. 'You will have bows in your hair, and I will brush it with the most beautiful brush made of gold.'

We walked for what seemed like hours, Claire entertaining me along the way, until we found an old abandoned farm hut. There, she lit a fire and told me to stay put. After a while she came back with goat's milk and heated it on the fire. She took a small amount of flour and water and cooked it in the coals. The milk was so very sweet and warm, and I dipped my bread in the milk, slurping up every morsel.

Then I saw Claire's foot. It was an unusual colour and looked sore. I massaged it with my hands to try and get the colour back into her skin, scolding her for not letting me know she was hurt. We lay by the fire for a long time, telling each other stories of what life could be and what our hopes and dreams were. Claire was only a young girl of around fourteen and I was about eight.

She loved my hair and tried her utmost to keep it free from knots, but one day it was so knotted she couldn't. I told her to cut it and reached into her small bag, handing her a knife.

'Cut it, Claire, cut it!' She cried as she did, and I hugged her tightly saying, 'It's only hair, nothing more.'

The scene changed as I continued into my meditation. I saw Claire laying on an old bed, a mattress of straw. She looked so pale and fragile.

She smiled and held my hand as she told me, 'Little One, soon I will have to leave you.'

Tears flowed down my cheeks, but I didn't say a word. Her breathing was laboured and I could feel her body struggling to cope.

There was an old man, Jacob, and his wife, Shallot, with us. They were kindly folk, farmers who owned a small plot of land.

Throughout the night I sat with Claire, cooling her brow with a damp cloth. Sometimes I lay beside her, gently touching her hair and face. Before the sun rose, Claire's body began to shudder. I held her hand, blood beginning to trickle from her mouth. I moved closer, turning her head so she wouldn't choke, but the blood came stronger. She looked at me one last time, then left her body.

I heard Claire whisper in my ear, 'This is why you silence when you are hurt. This is the reason it is easy for you to become silent, Little One. The grief has been there for many years, for lifetimes. It has connected to your DNA and needs to be released. Your love for me was at a soul level. Each time you lose people your psyche relates to this time of great grief.'

I stayed with her for hours. I didn't talk, my little heart and mind just didn't want to let her go. Jacob and Shallot knew I needed this time with Claire, so they waited and let me stay with her. Eventually we buried her on their plot of land. For weeks I didn't speak. Often, Jacob would come collect me from her grave.

He would take my hand and say, 'Come, Little One, our body needs food.'

He was such a kind man. I stayed with him as he watched his beloved wife, Shallot, die of the same illness as Claire.

At some point in the vision I saw I had grown and married. Jacob had raised me as his daughter. I was happy, but I could never say Claire's name without being touched by great sadness. Then I was on my deathbed surrounded by those I loved.

I saw Claire come to me in spirit and she took my hand.

Those at my bed saw me smiling as I said, 'Claire, I love you.'

Then my spirit left its body. I was gone, and Claire and I were reunited in spirit.

Coming out of the vision, it took me awhile to stabilise mentally, emotionally and physically. I sat in the garden to ground myself back into this world, taking in all I had experienced. Many things came to me. I was not called 'Little One' by my guides because I was small, it was Claire's special name for me!

Claire was now at my side in the garden and I heard her say, 'We are bonded by our souls. You had to see the end of our life together, Little One, to see how deeply we loved each other and how hard your loss was to live with.'

'But I don't see you that age, Claire. I'm confused.'

'We have had three lives together, Little One. You see me now as I was in the last life. We will progress through these lives at a future time. But our first life together and your reaction to my death meant you were to go through many lessons. You continued to progress through many lives long after I became spirit.

'I needed you to know why you are called this name and why you can be so silent. Why you find comfort in not speaking. It was how you coped with our separation. I chose to guide you in this lifetime, because you were destined to watch those you love die, just as you did me. Do not be sad, my Little One. We had such great love and we still do. I will never leave you, just as you have never left me. We are bonded by our souls. When the time comes for you to leave your world and step into my world, my hand will be the first you grasp. I will watch over your children, just as I have watched over and loved my Little One. You have done well, my Little One. Now, rest.'

The following year, on the last day of what I have dubbed The Pomegranate Retreat, Claire came to me.

She said, 'Little One, we will sit together now. You have worked very hard and have seen things that have been very difficult for you to process. But now I want to show you our mother in the life we lived together. We had such joy in our life. You looked more like our mother and I resembled our father. Look now, Little One. See how we lived and how much we were loved.'

I saw a woman who was only young, with fair skin and long hair pulled into a bun at the nape of her neck. She was smiling and her eyes sparkled with delight.

I heard Claire whisper, 'She loved us dearly and so did our father.'

In spring our mother would take us for walks. I saw an image of her reaching for fruit from a tree. It tasted so sweet to my young mouth. Then, I saw us sitting in the grass eating blackberries, our fingers stained from the fruit. Sometimes the stain would take a few days to disappear, but we didn't care. Her name was Elizabeth, but my father called her Lizbet. Our father was a big, burly man with beautiful, kind eyes. I saw him lift her into his arms, twirling her in circles.

'You are lighter than a cloud and more beautiful than the sky you float in, Lizbet.' He loved her dearly.

I saw a game drawn in the dirt, a circle with partitions, each segment with a symbol and a stone in it. All the children had bags of stones and skipped around the circle until my mother said, 'Stop.' The children were laughing as each one was asked to leave because they had stopped on the wrong segment. I could feel the joy as I watched the game play out.

I was now at a table eating sweet bread and drinking warm milk for my breakfast. My name was Bethany but our mother called me Bethy.

She looked at me and said, 'Why, Bethy! You slept and changed overnight.'

I scrunched up my face and looked at her confused, wondering what she was talking about.

'Why, Bethy, you have changed into a traveller who has seen many places near and far. Great mountains and rolling plains. Flowers of all descriptions, creeks and rivers. All these things you have seen.'

I'd answer her with a look of utter surprise on my face.

'But I haven't, I'm sure I haven't changed and seen all these things.'

Each morning, she would greet me in this way as I came to the table: 'Now, you are woman of fine wares and servants to wait on you hand and foot. Oh, but what a fine horsewoman you have become. Racing faster than light with such courage in your heart.'

She would sit with me, explaining what I had become while I had slept soundly in my bed, I would listen wide-eyed and amazed at all she could see me become.

Then, with anticipation, I'd ask, 'What have I become today, Mother?' I could see Claire smiling as she waited for our mother to answer.

She took my face in her hands and said, 'Bethy, you are the most wonderful girl who could do anything with her life – because you are you, and I love you dearly.' Then she would kiss my forehead and ask me to eat my bread.

Elizabeth worked hard. Her hands were small, but rough from the life she lived. One day she had returned from visiting neighbours who were ill and had come home weary.

Our father wasn't happy she had been where she had saying, 'You are a very foolish woman Lizbet, with a heart that is too kind.'

But we knew he was only worried about her because he loved her so dearly.

She began to get strong fevers, and a woman was called to tend her ailment as our father sat at her side, cooling her forehead with a damp cloth. The fevers became worse. Eventually her body could take no more and she died. She looked so beautiful lying on the bed, her long hair flowing over her shoulders. We were each given a lock of her hair tied by twine.

Our father was devastated by her death. He tried to make sure we had enough to eat and cared for us girls each day. But soon he succumbed to drinking, as his grief became too much to bear. He became sullen and belligerent, not able to cope without the woman he loved. His once kind eyes had lost their spark. He had lost his true love along with his love of life.

Before long, Claire and I were to be on our own in the world.

Coming out of the meditation, Claire was at my side. 'This retreat was always going to be very difficult for you. You will need some time to assimilate back into your daily life when you return from retreat. But I wanted you to see the joy we experienced in that life together. I wanted you to know you were very much loved, just as you were by your own mother and grandmother in this life. And you still are, to this day. We will talk of our other lives at a later time.' She smiled and said, 'But now you must eat the pomegranate we guided you to bring. The hard work is over.'

The Pomegranate Retreat was one of the most difficult retreats I had ever undertaken. But it was, as all my retreats are, very necessary. It left me feeling mentally, physically and emotionally exhausted. Claire has always been there at my side, through all I go through on retreat. Just as she has in my day to day life and wanted to make sure I also had some joyful memories of this retreat. This beautiful woman has been my rock throughout my life, in fact a number of my lives. I will always love her deeply, just as she has loved her Little One. I have no doubt, just as she has said she will be there to greet me when eventually it is my time to leave this earth plane and join the world of spirit.

My guides have always been a beautiful constant in my life and I will be forever grateful for their presence. They are by my side teaching me and helping me discover the many lessons life brings toward me as I walk this earth. They have always shown me such patience and compassion. When I don't 'get' a particular lesson, they are there at my side to console and let me know there is always time to learn.

We will continue to learn until our last breath. And if you may be 'slow learners' like this Little One, then there are always lifetimes ahead to continue our soul studies.

People often say I have been given a gift that is truly remarkable. But to be quite honest, I have never called what I'm able to do, a gift. I see the true gift that I have been given as being My People in spirit, my beautiful guides. I will always feel blessed for this gift that I can only describe as soul love. That gift of soul love is a gift like no other. I am truly blessed to have them in my life.

Chapter Six

HE WHO HUNTS

Let me show you my world of brown and green,
Of places your eyes have never really seen.

A place in nature, a path, the water, the trees.
The way the wind touches you embraced by the breeze.

Our feet touching the earth so softly, so gently.
Our eyes always watching our surroundings intently.

A ray of sunshine from above pinpoints such a beautiful scene,
Showing us Mother Nature is surely our queen.

A single leaf floating down from the sky.
All is quiet as we watch the birds up high.

One moment in time, there is so much detail to see,
If only you take the time to just be.

Oringo

I have had many guides step forward to teach and guide me along my path. Some stay for a short time and others stay with me for many years. All are important to my growth and my work with Spirit.

Oringo has only been with me for a few years, but we have formed a bond which can only be described as unique. When this beautiful man in spirit stepped forward, I immediately was drawn to his broad smile and sparkling eyes.

His name, Oringo, means 'he who hunts.' He has very dark skin, a mop of thick black hair and a thin, muscular physique. He showed me he was both the hunter and protector of his tribe when he was on the earth plane.

One of the first things he ever said to me was, 'Little One, it is important you learn the value of a single moment and the detail within that moment. This is what I will teach you.'

When Oringo first came to me he showed me how to see in detail and asked me to settle my mind. He talked about how he would protect his tribe by bringing attention to himself, leading the perceived threat away from those he protected, his tribe. Then when he was followed, he would hide in the forest.

'Little One, see if you can find Oringo. But you must concentrate to do this.'

I watched in my mind as he led those who cause danger away from his tribe, and followed his path as he moved through the forest. Within what seemed like seconds, he disappeared. I couldn't see him anywhere. Then I remembered his words, asking me to concentrate. So I began scouring the forest for signs of where he was. But I as hard as I tried, I just couldn't find him.

Then, Oringo rose from the earth, his hiding place, and looked at me intensely. I gasped, shocked at the fact I had no idea he was hiding there. Then his face spread into the broadest grin I had ever seen and he began laughing.

'See, Little One, I became invisible. I will teach you to be invisible.'

Oringo had covered himself in dirt and undergrowth from the forest. Not once did he move under all that debris from the forest. Not one thing seemed to point to where he was hiding. He had, as he said, become invisible. This was how he protected his tribe.

He was there to teach me that the smallest detail is important, and to see that detail you must always look with all your senses. There are always things that us humans miss because we are too busy in the mind, and this leads to being too busy in our lives. So we miss those fine details of life.

Oringo comes forward often and we have become very close. He has the most wonderful sense of humour and makes me laugh often. But all my guides are with me for a reason and Oringo is no exception. He will often come to my side if I'm working on a missing person case or if I need information in a reading that entails hidden details. He is also a great help when I'm driving to a location I'm not familiar with or just feel nervous about the journey.

I remember the first time I drove to the Gold Coast to see my daughter and granddaughter. For some reason I had always had a fear of this huge bridge I had to drive over. I just didn't like the energy of this bridge.

As I was driving towards it, I heard Oringo say from the passenger seat, 'Ahh, the scary bridge, Little One.'

And yes, that's what I actually called it.

'Little One, this road is no different to other roads. It is your fear invading the mind.'

I knew that but I still didn't like it.

'We will conquer this scary bridge. Think of it like you are going on an amusement ride, like a rollercoaster ride.'

I looked at him and said, 'Oringo, I don't like rollercoasters.' I rolled my eyes as though to say, *You should know that.*

He looked at me and began laughing. I also chuckled a bit.

'Okay, okay, but we are now on the top of this road Little One and you are still alive. Isn't this true?'

I nodded and as we were going down the other side of the bridge, I felt my fear fade. He was right, I had created the fear in my head.

Oringo was laughing and his eyes sparkled as he clapped.

'See? This is no scary bridge.'

I smiled as I looked at Oringo's face, so childlike, filled with positivity. And yes, that's the last time I called it the Scary Bridge. My new name for it is the No Longer Scary Bridge.

He looked at me with those dark intense eyes of his and said in a serious tone, 'Little One, remember Oringo is here for you, I will never allow danger to be near you. We are one. We journey together.'

Oringo continued to guide me along my car journey. He would tell me to stay in this or that lane and make me aware of drivers who were careless. On the way home, I was just merging onto the highway, feeling quite confident and happy with myself. I thought I was doing pretty darn good!

Then, I heard Oringo say strongly, 'Little One, go to left. Go to left lane now!'

I did as he said, wondering what the problem was. Within minutes, I saw a trailer up ahead come away from its car and it was now sideways on the lane I had been travelling on. Cars were skidding to a stop! We drove past the dumbfounded driver who was now out of his car, shaking his head in disbelief.

Then Oringo said, 'No danger now, Little One. Relax, we are going home.'

I smiled and knew Oringo and I would always be a great team.

Part of my training with Oringo involves him taking me into forests and teaching me to see in detail what each forest holds. He is extremely patient with me and often uses his humour to get a point across to his Little One.

I remember the first walk I ever went on with him and how before starting off, he asked me to always trust him.

'Remember, Oringo is with you. Let fear go, do not be like the deer and scurry here and there. We walk slowly, gently. Do not disturb the earth.'

Upon entering the forest, we stopped so Oringo could ask permission to enter from the owners of the land. An Aboriginal man in spirit nodded to me in recognition, letting me know I was welcomed.

We began to walk and I felt the energy of the place. It was very quiet and so beautiful. Massive trees surrounded us and I wondered how ancient they must be. They looked like they had been there since time began.

'Little One, you walk the body for exercise, not for seeing. Stop. You must slow to at least half your pace.'

The Aboriginal man chuckled. 'She hurry, hurry,' he said to Oringo.

'Okay, okay, I guess I was walking like I'm exercising. I agree.'

Oringo leaned closer and whispered in my ear, 'You also walk like elephant, Little One.'

I looked at him a little surprised. 'What?'

'You will scare the forest people away before you see them if you walk like elephant.' Oringo grinned and put his hands in the air as much as to say, 'It's true.'

Geez, this forest walking was harder than I thought it would be!

'Now breathe, and walk slowly, gently. As though you are becoming invisible to the world you are in, our world, the forest.'

I stopped and focused on the moment and my path. I began to step forward lightly, gently, watching where I placed each step. I slowed and became more aware of my surroundings and the sounds of the forest.

'Ah, that's better, slowly, slowly. See what is missed when there is hurry in your steps?'

I began to feel the forest energy more strongly and it felt good to feel this energy. I became aware of the different calls from the birds high up in the forest canopy and was trying to work out where they were.

Oringo whispered, 'The forest echoes their calls, Little One. Each call bounces off the trees. The birds are very high up. Look for the branches they hide amongst.'

I scoured the branches, listening to the birds. I finally focused on one branch and looked at Oringo for approval.

He shook his head and grinned, 'Close, but no. Remember this is your first walk. We will concentrate only on walking softly and seeing today.'

'Come sit with us, Little One.' I sat on a huge fallen tree and wondered why it had fallen. 'Look up now.' My gaze went toward the canopy of the forest. 'Watch, now. Be in the moment.' One single leaf began to gently float down from the canopy. 'Stay with this leaf's journey.'

I concentrated only on the leaf as it made its way down from above. Time seemed to have stopped. All I could see was one single leaf, everything else had faded. Until finally it landed at my feet.

'Yes, this is good. This is how you see in our forest world, Little One.' Oringo was grinning and the Aboriginal man was nodding in approval. 'Come, let us move on now.'

As I walked, I became aware of so many things that I had missed earlier on when I was apparently walking like an exercising elephant. Mosses and fungi growing on the trees. Some of the fungi looked like shells that had implanted themselves on the bark of the trees. Branches and vines that were twisted and reaching toward the sun. Small brightly coloured insects, and spider webs that seemed to be enhanced by the dappled sunlight.

Something touched my neck and I jumped, startled.

Oringo leaned forward and whispered in my ear, 'Calm, Little One. This is just killer leaf from tree.'

I turned and looked at him and saw that unique Oringo grin spread across his face and I chuckled. *Darn killer leaves need to understand I'm only a novice forest walker and they need to stay clear of my energy.*

That became a running joke with Oringo every time I walked with him. Each time we would enter a forest, he would grab my shoulders and look deeply into my eyes saying very seriously, 'Little One, remember Oringo will protect you from the killer leaves. Do not fear!' Then he'd break out in that enormous smile of his and we'd laugh.

Coming out of the forest, I was a little disappointed I hadn't seen any birds up close. I'm very much a bird woman since I had bonded with my magpies. Oringo must've read my thoughts and told me to stop and be very still.

'Look, Little One, watch them play.'

I looked to where he was pointing and saw five fairy wrens moving from branch to branch in the forest undergrowth. I always take my phone with me when walking to capture photos of different things I see. My hand went to reach for my phone, but Oringo stopped me.

'Do you want to capture these birds in your phone or experience them now so they are forever in your mind and heart?'

I let go of the need to capture them and knew it was better to just be with them in that moment. We sat and watched them for about twenty minutes. Oringo was right, I have held that experience in my mind and heart and it has never faded.

Returning to my retreat house, I made myself a cup of tea and sat out on the deck. I watched the trees and different birdlife, and how they moved throughout the forest that backed onto the house. Annan, another guide I have, sat by my side as I processed my walk with Oringo. It was so peaceful looking at the trees sway with the breeze and listening to the sounds of the birds.

My ears began to focus in on a sound to the left of where I was sitting and my eyes tried to focus on the area the noise was coming from. It took a while, but I finally focused on both the area and the sound. Yet, I still couldn't see the bird I was sure was in that area.

I asked, 'Where is the bird, Annan?'

He replied, 'This is not my area, Little One, you must ask Oringo.'

I was slightly surprised at his answer.

Oringo stepped forward and leaned in, whispering, 'Annan is correct. This is not why he is here with you. Little One, yes, the area is correct and you have done well to pick up this noise. But the noise you hear is no bird. Look up. See the wire that moves with breeze?'

I did as he said. I could then see the wire he was talking about.

Oringo poked me gently in the ribs and grinned. 'This is the noise you hear, this is your bird, but wire is not bird.'

I looked at him dumbfounded and then we both began laughing. Apparently this Little One needs a lot more forest teaching.

Oringo has been on many retreats with me. Each time I walk the forest with him I gain greater insight into how his forest world works and what it can teach me. I have come to love this man dearly and know he holds such wisdom.

As I snuggled down into my bed the first time Oringo worked with me, he came forward and drew a symbol on my forehead. and smiled as he looked deeply into my eyes. I saw in my mind's eye, there was an arc and then a small wavy line underneath, then below the line was what I thought was a number eight. He explained his symbol in a soft gentle voice as he sat on my bed.

'Little One, this arc is Oringo and the line below is you. The symbol below is not a number. It means infinity. I place this on your forehead to show you I have covered you. I will protect you, Little One, for infinity. You will always be safe. Now sleep deeply, we have much to do.'

I continue to work with Oringo and he helps me in so many ways, including, helping me find someone who is lost, teaching me to see in detail, and understanding the natural world and what it can teach me.

Why have I dedicated a chapter to Oringo? I do this because even though Claire and My Indian have been wonderful constants in my life, I have had so many different spirit guides come into my life over the years, each one with something different to teach me. Each has their own unique, beautiful energy and personality. All My People in spirit are part of the team who help me to live out my calling as a clairvoyant medium to the best of my ability. Each one also teaches me what I need to know about myself as I walk my path in this life. I am eternally grateful they walk beside me each and every day.

Oringo has taught me some important lessons that nature holds. If we are in sync with nature, it can heal us in many profound ways. He has shown me how seeing in detail is done by being totally in the moment, and how much we miss if we rush and scatter our senses. He taught me that laughter is always necessary as we walk our path through life, and that walking like an elephant is really only going to work well for elephants. If we take each step softly and gently on this earth, it will always bring better results.

Chapter Seven

A Mother's Wish

So many times, I dreamed of having you in my arms.
Of holding your tiny body close to my heart.
A precious bundle of joy, tiny fingers and toes.
And because of you, I pushed aside all of my worries and qualms.

You were always my greatest wish
To be your mother
The most important role I was to ever play.
My desire for you I could never once dismiss.

The smell of your soft, downy hair.
So many times I watched you sleep.
Your laughter and sweet little grin.
Your angelic face, there was nothing that could compare.

My darling one, you came into my heart.
A tiny bundle of joy that changed my days.
You became my life, my world.
And from that moment on I knew we would never truly part.

You are my child, this day and every day.
And though death may call at some point in time,
Remember my beautiful wish, my one desire.
Our bond as mother and child cannot be broken and will forever stay.

A Mother's Wish

To be blessed with a child is one of the greatest gifts you can ever receive. From conception to when that child is placed in your arms. To the days, months or years they are under your care and guidance. As a mother, your child is never far from your mind. That precious child becomes your whole world and no one could ever replace them.

I remember when my own two beautiful children came into my world and how everything in my life changed. Being the 'I can do anything' sort of woman I am, I thought I could easily handle being a mum. Mind you, by no means did I have rose-coloured glasses on. I knew there would be challenges. But oh, how wrong I was thinking I could handle motherhood like a duck to water!

From the first moment I laid eyes on my firstborn I loved him with all my heart and soul. He became my life. But someone forgot to tell me babies don't always sleep! In fact, my precious little boy almost never slept and if he did it was on my chest. I think he liked the sound of his mother's heart beat, it soothed him.

I was so sleep deprived I looked ill. To make matters worse, the only relief I got was when my own mother came to give me a break. His father worked away most days, only coming home on weekends if he could.

But oh, how I loved him, and before long I was expecting his little sister. A wide-eyed, tiny little girl with a shock of dark hair. Now, even though she was tiny, she still made a huge impact on my body while I was carrying her. For the last three months of pregnancy I had to lay down and rest to rid my body of fluid that was building up.

Well, to lay down and do nothing tested my patience to no end! But my own mother was there every day, encouraging me to rest and making sure I wasn't doing anything.

If she heard me get up I'd hear, 'Trine, we are supposed to be resting, remember?'

'Yes Mum, I know.'

And I'd scamper back into bed like a naughty child, wondering how she knew I was out of bed when she was in the lounge room at the other end of the house. I know now that a mother's intuition doesn't ever really cease, even when your child is a fully grown adult.

My beautiful children are chalk and cheese in all aspects. One born with strawberry blonde hair and the fairest skin. The other with black hair and beautiful olive skin, like her grandfathers in spirit. Their personalities are so different, no one would know they are brother and sister – but they are! And I have no doubt, that as siblings they will teach each other many life lessons throughout their journeys. And I will always see myself as the luckiest person on this earth to be chosen as their mumma.

I have always loved children. They have such a wonderful way of looking at the world and all it offers us. I often think that as we grow older, we forget to retain that vital part of us, the child within. As adults, we get bogged down in the busyness of life. Work, family obligations and day to day responsibilities seem to take up much of our time. We forget to stop and play. We forget to cherish those simple, yet often extraordinary moments like a child does.

Throughout my time as a clairvoyant medium, I have done many readings for mothers. Often these mothers bring in photos of their precious children so I can guide them to help their child develop and grow in the best way. My grandmother taught me at a young age to look at photographs and 'see' what information came to me. I only ever read photographs of living people, because it's my job as a medium to describe the physical traits of the dead to my client.

I have also sat across from many grief-stricken parents and endeavoured to show them their child lives on in spirit. I have seen how difficult it is for them to understand why their precious child is no longer with them here on Earth. I have also seen the comfort and joy that fill their hearts as they realise their child is with them in spirit each and every day. Their child trying to help them live on and come to terms with the grief they are feeling.

I love reading for children in spirit. The images of where they are in spirit are always so beautiful and colourful. Spirit shows me they are always greeted by those they love, a grandparent or a relative in spirit will take them by the hand and show them the beauty that is in the afterlife. They will make sure their passing from this life into the next life is a positive and calm transition.

Each reading is different, and unfortunately, I can never promise I can communicate with the person my client wishes to connect with in spirit. But with the help of my guides, we try to prove to my client that those they love, live on in spirit. That sometimes means another person in spirit will come through to show my client their child is content and happy in the world of spirit. When another person acknowledges the presence of a child in spirit they often come forward with their arms in the cradling position, symbolically holding a child.

I have been able to connect many mothers with their children in spirit and I absolutely love these readings. I can think of no harder death to come to terms with than the death of a precious child. Whether that child died in the womb, or lived an hour, a week, a year, or until an adult, their death will still be devasting to the parents, but especially to the mother.

I have included three very special spirit children in this chapter. I could have included many more, but these three have always stuck in my mind and their beautiful mothers have given me permission to tell their stories in this book.

I admire all these wonderful women. They have shown grace, strength and courage in the face of such a devastating loss. But I know without a doubt, these three mothers know their precious child is by their side in spirit, giving them the strength to go on.

My Beautiful Rose

Many years ago, a young dark-haired woman nervously sat down with me for a reading. I explained how I do my readings (as I always do with any client that comes to me) and tried to help her relax with a bit of Trina humour. I often use humour in my readings as I know my clients are dealing with a great depth of sorrow, frustration and confusion. Their emotions are often raw and fragile, and a touch of gentle humour seems to help them relax.

I began to concentrate on who was coming in from spirit for this young woman. There was an older lady stepping forward and I began to describe her in detail. The woman nodded, knowing who it was and seemed pleased that she was there for her. But then a young child came through and looked at me with such intensity I was taken aback.

A beautiful child of about four years old, she had the most gorgeous brown eyes that seemed to look right through me. I thought to myself, *Is she angry? Why is she looking at me like I'm in trouble?*

But My People in spirit whispered in my ear, 'Little One, describe the child to your client.'

I said, 'I have a little girl here with the most beautiful eyes and she would be about four. But this little girl has the most intense gaze, it's like she's looking at me to say she means business and I'm in trouble. She's very strong willed.'

My client stiffened and seemed to be waiting for more.

The little girl then smiled and her whole face seemed to change. She was beautiful. She whispered in my ear, 'Sing Happy Birthday.'

Again, I was a little taken aback. I was not a singer. In fact, many people have suggested I stick to my dancing as apparently my voice isn't that of an angel.

I said to her in my mind, *Why Happy Birthday? Why do you want me to sing?*

She sighed impatiently and said again, 'Sing Happy Birthday. Sing it over and over again, it's important.'

Well I decided not to hurt my client's ears by singing and instead said, 'The little girl says I must sing Happy Birthday over and over again as it's important to you. Do you understand what she's saying?'

I could see the young woman becoming emotional and I asked if she was okay as her eyes were filling with tears.

At this point the little girl piped up with 'I love pancakes too.'

I passed the message on as that is what I'm trained to do. As a medium, it is our job to pass on word for word what those in spirit are saying to the client. Then I saw an image of roses and thought maybe she wanted to give her roses as a gift. I explained what I saw.

The little girl then said, 'She's my mummy, and I have a brother too.'

The mother explained that her daughter had died at four from leukemia. And yes, every day they would sing her Happy Birthday as she loved to blow out the candles on a cake. Her brother was very close to her and she loved to make pancakes with her daddy. The little girl's name was Rose.

Little Rose went on to describe that she is often with her younger sister, because the younger sister could be a bit naughty. Her mother laughed and agreed she was definitely a handful. I was enjoying my interaction with little Rose and was pleased the mother knew without a doubt it was her daughter. But I was still confused with how Rose came to me at the start of the reading.

'Why did she give me such a dirty look when she first came through?'

The mother laughed and said her daughter was only four, but when the nurses or doctors came in she would give them this filthy look. Rose was known for this look and everyone would comment on how it made them a little nervous when they approached her.

I laughed and said, 'Yep, I can see how they would be a bit afraid of this feisty four-year-old and her fierce look.'

All Rose ever talked about when she was alive was going to school and how she was looking forward to all the things she could do at school. Unfortunately Rose never got to go to school on Earth. But she explained to her mother that she gets to go to school in spirit and she loves everything about it.

As the years went on I continued to read for not only Rose's mother, but her father and grandmother too. And as the years passed, I saw little Rose grow up in spirit.

Just as children here on Earth grow each year, so do children in spirit. When it is time for those that are left behind on Earth to eventually pass to spirit, they will be shown the child at the age they died, and then how they have grown in spirit. I have no doubt that my beautiful Rose will continue to watch over her family from spirit, guiding them the best way she can.

My Smiling Bike Boy

As I welcomed my client I could immediately sense her nervousness. She was a petite woman with blonde hair and a lovely, friendly energy. But as she followed me into my work room, I knew this reading would be significant. I could feel My People in spirit strongly. I could also feel the lady's energy and her grief, but I steadied myself and began to read.

I immediately saw a bicycle and told her, 'I need to put this in your lap.'

Her face crumbled and I could see it meant something to her, but still asked if she understood.

She replied, 'Yes' in a quiet, shaky voice.

I could see someone riding fast with his head down, concentrating on what he was doing as he rode along the road. He seemed very fit and even though my own mother rode a bike, I knew this person was more competitive. He meant business!

Then I felt an impact. I was a bit confused. *What happened?*

Often in a reading, I need to become the person who has passed to understand what is happening. This does not mean I have to feel all their distress, but it can help me tell my client more about what transpired.

I could see a young man who had the most gorgeous smile. He was thin, with tousled hair and a pale complexion. I could feel the effort in his body as he rode and knew he was extremely good at what he did. But as he was riding, a car hit him and his lifeless body was on the ground. It was instant. I saw his spirit leave his body. He looked confused, trying to understand why he wasn't in his body anymore. All this seemed to be happening in a dream state.

I went back to the young man standing beside me and he said, 'I couldn't get back in my body, so I went looking for Mum. I knew she would be devastated.' I could feel the love he had for his mother as he looked at her. 'We were very close, and when I was alive, I believed in what you do. I always knew we lived on after death. Mum and I would often talk about this subject.'

His mother told me they would often spend time together watching the celebrity medium John Edward on television.

He showed me medals and that he was always riding, trying to improve his skills.

The lady sitting in front of me was now crying and I knew this young man was her son. But I stopped and asked if she was okay, and if she recognised the person I was describing.

'Yes, he's my son and was killed by a car as he was riding his bicycle in training.'

I could see the car and an older man at the wheel. He hadn't seen the young man and really shouldn't having been driving at his age.

She passed me a group photo of her close family which also had five of her nieces and nephews in the photograph. Immediately I saw the young man standing next to me and pointed to him in the picture.

'That's him,' I said. 'That's his beautiful smile. That's exactly how I see him.'

She told me his name was Scott and he had won several trophies for cycling. I saw an image of Cadell Evans, a professional cyclist. I knew young Scott was somehow connected or could have been as good as him as a cyclist. But then Scotty (as I call him, because of that cheeky grin and his playful energy) became serious.

He said, 'Tell her I don't want that thing in her lap.'

I was a little confused about what he was talking about, but passed the message on and said, 'He's very adamant about this.'

'It's just not me,' he said.

The mother then explained she had discussed funeral arrangements with her husband late one night. She had said

A Mother's Wish

to him, 'I would like Scott to be cremated, so that way at least I could hold him in my lap.'

She had only discussed this with her husband, no one else was in the room. I knew young Scotty was showing her proof of survival. Part of my job as a medium is to show those you love in spirit watch over you. Yes, their body is dead, but their spirit and the love they have for you lives on in the afterlife.

He talked of his dog who passed over after him and that the dog was with him. He spoke about how his father would help him with his cycling training. How it would be difficult for him to step away from the sport Scott loved, and probably wouldn't for some time. His sister also cycled, but she needed to train harder. And of his brother who was as dedicated to the sport as he had been, but felt it difficult to continue now he was gone.

He explained there would be things dedicated to him in the future and how the family would eventually heal. Cadell Evans later helped the family set up a foundation named after Scott for cyclists and donated a signed jersey that raised quite a lot of money for the foundation. Scott's cycling community also have a memorial race each year and have helped many up and coming cyclists.

Before long, it felt like Scotty was a friend and we were just having a chat. I loved his energy. But I also knew his family would take a very long time to heal from this tragedy. I saw my own father's death and knew Scott must have died close to Christmas.

His mother told me he died on 15 December. On that day, she had heard the Christmas presents being rattled and couldn't work out what the noise was all about. Scott's father had also had a premonition about his son's death. He had rung his wife in the afternoon telling her of his fear their son had been killed. Scott hadn't had any identification on him when he was killed. Later that day his employer rang his father to tell him Scott hadn't turned up for work and he had heard of an accident involving a cyclist. His father then contacted police and sadly it was their beloved son who had been killed. Scott had died at 10 o'clock that morning.

When Scott's spirit realised he was no longer alive, his first thought was, 'I must get to Mum – she will be devastated.'

I have no doubt in my mind Scott had returned to the family home from spirit, to make sure his loved ones were okay on the day of the tragedy.

There have been many times throughout the years I have seen my young cyclist, Scotty. And every time I do, he has a beautiful smile on his dial. He was a beautiful boy who had a passion and gift for cycling. He was a compassionate and loving boy who always believed there was an afterlife. He was determined to reach for his goals and had his loving family's support. But on that day, his life was taken away by one foolish act, driving when you cannot see in detail. It's a tragedy that should never have happened, but it did.

I'm sure Scott's family have learned many lessons not just from his life, but also his death. They will be forever grateful he was a special part of their family, even if it was only for a short time.

My Little River Boy

When I first started to assemble the components of this book together, I knew I wanted to include some of my spirit children. Rose and Scott came to mind immediately, but as I was writing I still felt something – or someone – was missing. I needed to include something else.

Writing the chapter titled 'This Is Me' I felt a familiar energy. There was a little boy in spirit close by. Tuning into this energy, I recognised it was a five-year-old boy in spirit I call

A Mother's Wish

my 'River Boy.' I thought, yes, I must include this little one. But I had a bit of a problem. As the readings with his mother were so long ago, the details were a bit sketchy in my mind. I remembered seeing dirty water and could see I was at the river. I knew this little fellow had died from drowning. It was the most tragic accident and was very difficult for the family to deal with. I remembered his cheeky grin. His name was Ross, or as his mother calls him, Rossy.

While living in my hometown, I had read for Yvonne many times. Since moving to Queensland, I had only read for her once a couple of years ago. But I distinctly remembered my little river boy coming in and showing me his passing was due to water. His energy was exactly the same as it was all those years ago.

It's very rare that I contact my clients, due to privacy ethics. So, I hesitantly typed out a text, explaining why I was contacting her and asking for permission to include her gorgeous little son in my book. I also asked why she knew without a doubt it was her son I brought forward in her reading. Hovering over the 'send' button, I still questioned if I was doing the right thing. I hit 'send', and before long I received a lovely heartwarming reply, giving me her permission to include her son in my book.

On receiving her text and the information she gave me, I realised I wanted to present his story in a somewhat different way. Why? Because her message showed how a death no matter how tragic, can also create change in someone's life path. It often leads people to go out and really discover who they are, to begin living the life they are meant to live.

Ross was your typical little boy, full of life and often the loudest in the room. In our last reading, I described information he passed on about his mother's grandchildren. He described how his favourite teddy had been given to them, a purple teletubby. She mentioned I had been on her mind and that her son must've been nudging her, just as he did myself. It was twenty years since his passing, with his birthday the next month. The 4th of May, the same birthdate as my own younger brother.

Images of past readings came into my mind, where I could see him affecting the lights in the family home. Light globes would blow and lights would flicker. I could see him running through the house, just as any living little boy would. He was full of excitement and not giving a damn about how much noise he was creating. His cheeky little smile lit up his face.

Yvonne, my river boy's mother, described him as her 'gift' child. This immediately touched something inside of me. She had sent me a piece she wrote on her business page, called 'Life is a Gift vs Death is a Gift.' As I read it, I began to understand her beautiful name for her child in spirit. He certainly was a gift.

Any child we are blessed with is a beautiful gift. But imagine having that beautiful gift you had loved for five years, taken from you in one tragic moment. I have no doubt the grief a mother experiences will stay with her for a lifetime.

It is often through experiencing a death that we come to know ourselves more intimately. Death forces us to look at our own life, how we are living, and can create positive change.

She wrote:

'As time went on, it became clear that my son's death was going to change my life in more ways than I could have imagined.

His gift to me – to see things I couldn't see before.

To hear and feel things I never knew existed.

Strength and courage to do things I never even dreamt of.'

Yvonne is now a practicing death doula. I have no doubt she will help many families come to terms with the final passage from this world to the next.

Her beautiful boy who was gifted to her at birth was full of life, and the time he spent on Earth was definitely a gift to his family and those that knew and loved him. But he also gave his mother the gift of truly seeing what she could become, even if he couldn't be physically by her side. He showed her from spirit, he lives on and is able to connect with her, even though they reside in two different worlds.

My little river boy has touched the lives of many. Not just in the short time he lived, but also after death. The universe often gives us the gift of seeing that.

Over the years, Yvonne has had people come to her and say, 'I have changed, because of your son's death. I have changed how I parent my children, because of your son's death.'

I have no doubt this beautiful little boy in spirit will continue to change the lives of others in years to come. But first, he needed to give a gift to the woman who gifted him life. He needed to show his mother who he loved so dearly, all the potential she had within herself. And he needed to give her the strength and courage to become who she was meant to be, so that she could change other people's lives.

Ross's life was a gift and his death was also a gift, given from his soul to his mother's soul.

The most beautiful thing about this, is Yvonne has no doubt in her mind that her son came to her as a gift and continues to be a gift that keeps giving long after the physical body is gone.

As I said earlier, to lose a child to death, no matter the length of time they were here, will always be devastating. But as a medium I do get to see them in spirit and how beautifully they are looked after by their loved ones in spirit.

Their world in spirit is magnificent. The little ones show me such vibrant colours and landscapes of where they live on. I see them laughing and playing with such joy and contentment. Their world in spirit is filled with love.

As a mother who hasn't lost a child, I cannot even begin to imagine how much grief these mothers carry within their hearts. But as a clairvoyant medium, I do know their child lives on in spirit. And I know when the time comes for you to pass from this earthly world to the world of spirit, you will be reunited again.

But for now, I hope you find peace in the knowledge you and your precious child are connected by a very special bond, the bond of love. And the bond of love cannot be broken, not even by death.

What have these beautiful children taught me and the ones they left behind? I have no doubt in my mind, these children have come to teach us that life is precious.

Each life we give birth to is gifted to us for a reason. These precious souls show us the importance of understanding what life is all about and how just a single moment can teach us many things.

I agree with my beautiful Rose, that each day we live should be greeted with joy and celebrated with as much gusto as we celebrate our yearly birthday. Life is sometimes too short to not appreciate each day we are given.

So, wear your special clothes whenever you wish. Use all those things you keep for special occasions. Tell those special people in your life you love them each and every day. Dance and sing to beautiful music in your lounge room. Take that holiday you've been thinking about. Eat that second piece of cake. Go out and live life to the fullest, because each day you wake and rise from your bed should always be celebrated, as though it is the best gift you will ever receive.

Chapter Eight

No Goodbyes

When I think of you, I remember so many things.
A smile, your eyes, the smell of your hair and the touch of your skin.
All these things touch deeply at my heartstrings.

A day when my world was changed forever.
Your time on this earth now done, finished.
My heart now breaking, knowing we can no longer be together.

Your soul was ready to fly, no time for goodbyes.
No last hugs or words to be said.
No longer in my arms, you now move amongst the wise.

Time will now always stand still.
In my mind, your face etched as I last saw you.
How can I go on? My grief sighs, knowing deep within I will.

But oh, how I wish we had one last day. Please, I need more time.
Time to say all my heart felt for you.
Now knowing I will miss you my whole lifetime.

Maybe your beautiful soul had learned all its lessons.
Decided, you had learned well and it was your time.
But my heart and mind still scream. Please, just a few more seconds.

Let me say at least one last goodbye.
Please let me tell you how much I love you and what you mean to me,
Before you fly towards that beautiful expanse of sky.

Death is inevitable. And each day we live, we draw closer and closer to that final time we call death!

Death happens to all of us. We cannot escape it. But death comes to us in many ways. Each death is as individual as the person who once lived. This means we deal with it in our own unique way. Processing the circumstances of that death and looking at emotions and thoughts regarding death, is part of the process. Then hopefully as we move through the process of grief, we come to terms with the loss we have experienced. But to some extent our lives will be forever changed.

I often say death is like a scar. The wound heals but we can still feel and see where the wound has occurred.

To lose a loved one without a goodbye can be extremely traumatic and cause its own problems. Sometimes that loss can be quick and without warning, such as through accidents. Other times, like in the case of a missing person, it can be drawn out over days, weeks or even years. There are too many scenarios for me to list here, but people who have experienced a death without a goodbye will understand the trauma and questions it leaves in your mind and heart. Questions and thoughts of 'If only', 'I should have', or 'Why didn't I?' In the midst of all this, the dominant thought will be 'Why?'

Over my time as a reader, I have had the privilege of reading for many people who have lost loved ones in tragic circumstances. These deaths have often been where there is no last kiss, hug, words or goodbyes. The grief can last a lifetime. But hopefully, we learn to go on living our own lives and remember the love that was shared and the love that continues from the world of spirit.

The Magnificent Man in His Flying Machine

As a daughter who lost her father to sudden death, I know how devastating this can be. No last goodbye, hug or smile, can be so hard to deal with. It can cause prolonged grief with many unanswered questions in one's mind.

During a reading, a beautiful young woman was sitting in front of me. She was not only beautiful in looks but I could feel she also had the most beautiful heart. A gentleman in spirit stepped forward and immediately I heard the song, 'Those Magnificent Men in Their Flying Machines' flow through my mind. I could feel the man's cheeky nature and how he was very intelligent. I told the woman the details of how he looked and that his death was sudden. But I was confused as to why his death actually occurred. I knew it was quick and it was an impact passing, but something didn't seem right. This man was very analytical in how he did things and very particular. He didn't like to make mistakes. I knew he was well known in his community and very well respected in his work.

Again, 'Those Magnificent Men in Their Flying Machines' played in my mind. I saw a Gladstone bag, which to me is a symbol of a father figure or being on the father's side of the family. I have always related the Gladstone bag as being synonymous with my own father, as he would often carry his beer bottles in this type of bag.

I explained that I was hearing the song but was confused as to why. I also wasn't actually seeing how he had passed into the world of spirit, even though I knew it was a sudden accident and there was no time for goodbyes.

As a clairvoyant medium, I may not be given the full amount of information I need to understand fully what spirit is trying to show me. I will admit this to my client when this is happening. The woman explained that the man I was describing was her father and he had died while flying his small airplane. It was very unexpected, as he was quite particular with anything to do with his love of flying.

I could see he had checked the plane before flying, as was his way and there seemed to be nothing of concern. Then he was in the air and the engine was making strange sounds and he was confused as to why. I could see he was annoyed, as he had been diligent when checking the plane before takeoff. He showed me newspaper articles and how he was very well known. I relayed this to the woman and she acknowledged it was correct.

This lovely father in spirit then showed me seeds. I looked at them, a little confused.

Then he said, 'Not the fruit, the seed.'

He was trying to show me what his nickname was and eventually I worked out the seeds were a pip. His nickname was Pip!

I have had the pleasure of reading for this young lady on a number of occasions. Later, I also had the opportunity to read for the gentleman's wife. Some of these readings have been focused on my mediumship and others have been focused on my clairvoyant abilities. Most times I will use both. Each time I read for this beautiful woman, her father always makes sure the energy is kept light and playful. I know this is because he wants his daughter to smile. Pip always comes across in my readings as a bit of a cheeky man who always was up for a joke and who kept people amused by his wicked sense of humour.

Each time I hear 'Those Magnificent Men in Their Flying Machines' in my mind, I know that Pip is nearby. I know his daughter or wife have something going on in their lives. It also means the man they loved so dearly has been watching over them and is letting me know me they will be contacting me soon for guidance.

Love never dies, and the bond they share lives on, even in death. I know without a doubt this cheeky gentleman with the dimpled smile will always be watching over his beloved family.

In my own mind, I imagine this beautiful father and husband still traversing the skies. But now, he is in no need of his magnificent flying machine. Now he is in spirit and owns the whole sky, free to soar wherever he wishes.

The Young Fisherman

I was sitting at my workspace when I knew something was up, and that I needed to check my Facebook page. I checked the notifications and noticed a lovely client had tagged me in post. I immediately thought, *What the heck is this all about?* I clicked on it and saw the post concerned a young man, who had gone missing on a fishing trip.

I was hesitant to look into this, but knew my lovely client always came from a place of love. I began to clairvoyantly read the situation and my guide Oringo stepped forward.

He said, 'Little One, you have always been able to get information quickly. It comes naturally to you. But now you must work differently. You must look more closely for details.'

Oringo told me each time I work on this, I must first look into his eyes. Doing this, I will be able to achieve the necessary level of concentration I would need to see every detail that is shown to me.

Oringo had only been with me for a short time, but I loved everything about him and what he could teach me. I looked into his deep brown eyes and immediately felt as though I was being pulled into another world, Oringo's world. A world where every little detail is magnified and showed in detail.

I saw this young man on a boat. I could feel his energy and all he stood for. He was a beautiful young man with a cheeky grin and soulful eyes. He was playful, yet very sensitive and insightful. I saw the details of that particular fishing trip play out.

I stepped away from what I was seeing and wondered what I should do with the information. I'm not a clairvoyant that likes to work in the spotlight. Even though I have worked on missing persons cases before, I felt hesitant to comment on the post. The family had posted they were open to hearing from psychics and the like, if they knew anything that would be helpful in finding him. I wasn't willing to post my findings like all the other psychics, clairvoyants and intuitive people, but I asked for a phone number. Within a short time, I had a phone number, but still I was hesitant to contact the person. Then I felt drawn to another person on the post. She was one of the people out searching for the young fisherman, so I privately messaged her and immediately she replied.

Again, I looked into Oringo's eyes and went into his world of detail. I could see the young fisherman feeling happy as he stepped onto his boat. It was a beautiful day. He was well versed in his ability as a fisherman and had a close connection with his family. He liked being out on the water because it felt big to him and he felt at ease on the water. He read the weather patterns well, especially when out in his boat. He was a responsible fisherman who always returned when he felt the weather was turning bad. This young man was no novice when it came to the water. He would never put himself in danger because he knew it may create worry for his family.

He was pleased with the sighting of a very large fish and had posted to a friend about this, but also annoyed his fish finder wasn't working well at that stage. He contemplated going north, then head off south-east. I could see co-ordinates on a compass. He seemed to have a gut instinct of larger fish. He was comfortable and relaxed at this stage and the boat headed in a somewhat of a diagonal direction.

I saw land to the right of him, no land in front and to the left land in the distance. I saw turtles going towards the land on the right. I saw sand on the land but also sticks like mangroves. He had stopped the boat and was sorting his fishing equipment. Then he started the boat, more going towards the top part of the land on the right. He turned to look over his left shoulder at what he thought was a sound in the water at the back of his boat.

I saw movement in the water, like a big fish. I saw the movie *Moby Dick* and realised this had to do with the symbology of a large fish. The boat was still running. I saw him casting his line, but he swore when he thought it wasn't a good cast or it was stuck on something.

In my vision he was standing and the boat was still running, which seemed to be very unlike what he would do normally. He realised the boat shouldn't be going and reached back to turn it off, but the boat became unsteady and he overbalanced. He was falling backwards and his head and side of his face connected with the boat as he fell into the water. He had something entangled around his leg and managed to free this. I could see he wasn't hurt badly. He was more shocked he was separated from his boat. I heard 'rookie mistake' and he was annoyed at himself. He looked toward the boat but knew he couldn't reach it so looked for the next best option, which was swimming to land.

I saw him starting to swim and even though he was confident in the water, to me, it seemed a long way away. He had to stop to look above the water to see it, but he was determined to get there. But he was frustrated with himself and concerned he would create worry for his family. He knew even if he reached land, it would still be a struggle for him and those that needed to find him.

His stomach and legs were aching from the effort it took, but he knew how the current worked and was trying to use this knowledge to help him reach land. Then I felt a rolling pain go through my body. Heat seemed to flow through every inch of my body. I knew something had stung him and had caused his body to react dramatically. But I then saw he had managed to reach wet sand and was trying to pull his body up closer to the dry sand so he was safe. He was moving in and out of consciousness.

When working on a missing person case, it is not just done in one session. It takes many sessions, often hours. Sitting and receiving and deciphering what is coming to you in all its many forms. This sort of work is a huge commitment and often it will invade your whole day.

I had been relaying my information to the person I started to call the 'searcher'. Each time I would give her information she would text back quickly and before long we had formed a special bond. She had become my Sammie Girl. I later found out that her best friend in spirit was the only one who ever called her that nickname. She once said we were meant to meet and the young fisherman made that happen. I believe without a doubt she is right. And as time went on with the search, my young fisherman often spoke of Sammie Girl with fondness.

I did chuckle at one stage when he informed me, 'You'll like Sammie, she's got the same sense of humour as you and she likes to have a drink.' Yep, nothing is secret when it comes to those in spirit!

When I informed my Sammie Girl of what he said, she replied, 'He's sure right about me liking a drink.'

By the second session, I knew my young fisherman wouldn't be found alive. He was already in the world of spirit before I had become involved. As I worked with him we also became bonded. We talked often, and still do! He was a very gifted skater and I remember having to do a reading not long after his death, which involved skateboarding. Well, I can tell you now, this little medium knows absolutely nothing about skateboarding!

As I was reading for a young gentleman, to my surprise my young fisherman walked in and said, 'I've got this Trina. Let me help you.'

And he indeed helped me! I understand skateboards a bit more now. But I had to laugh when he said in the reading, 'Trina, this guy doesn't do it like me, he just does the basics and isn't very good at even that.'

As I became more involved with the young fisherman, unusual things began happening with our lights in the house. One night, all the lights in the house wouldn't work at all, yet there seemed to be nothing amiss with the electricity. And we were the only ones in our street without lights! I mentioned to my partner that I thought it had to do with the young fisherman and he agreed. The lights came back on the next morning. We called our electrician but they couldn't find anything.

I had become completely focused on this case, to the point Oringo would not let me read that day as I had become extremely tired.

'Little One, you must step away today. Your mind and body are too tired. I will not allow you to look into my eyes today. Now rest!'

Begrudgingly, I stepped away and lay on my bed, watching a movie with my partner. But this young fisherman was on my mind. I was feeling the depth of sorrow his family must have been feeling. Suddenly, the light above us came on and then turned off. Now, this light can only be turned on at the wall switch.

My partner looked at me, asking 'The fisherman?'

'Yep. I was just thinking about him.'

He shook his head and grinned. We also had another incident with our lights before I finished working on his case.

My partner loves me dearly and is very supportive when it comes to my work with Spirit. He is always ready to help in any way he can. I was very confused with the co-ordinates I had been given and he saw my frustration. I just don't do that sort of thing well. So, I gave him the co-ordinates and he showed me how to work them. It ended up being exactly where I had pointed to on the maps.

I read the young fisherman's disappearance for a number of days, and he showed me how he woke the following day he had reached the wet sand and was laying on his stomach. He looked up to a light that I think was the sun. His body was extremely weak, but he knew he had to get to somewhere higher. So, he hauled his body and placed himself in the fork of what looked like a mangrove. He was very ill, and I could feel in my own body that his heart and lungs were struggling. The next day, his body was in water for the second time. He was now in spirit.

The search was finally called off, the body not found.

This young fisherman was to be a catalyst for change. His death brought people together near and far for a common good. His impact in life and death will be felt for many, many years. I will remember him as a soldier of love. He created love in his life and allowed others to see the power of love in whatever they do.

After the search was called off, I wanted to continue reading his disappearance. But my main guide Claire told me it was time to step back, as I could do no more to help the situation. Me, being the stubborn person I am, didn't want to at all! Then the young fisherman stepped forward.

'I'm okay, Trina. You did more than enough, but not enough to save me. We connected in death and you could not do any more. Tell Mum I didn't hurt, it was like falling asleep. Tell her she did everything she could and was the best mum ever. Peace to my brother. I'll turn the lights on when I need you Trina and thank you.'

Although I had never met him while he was alive, this young fisherman has made a huge impact on myself and many others. And yes, his death was just as he described. It was like falling asleep in the arms of someone you love. Then he was greeted and embraced by those he loved in spirit.

The one thing I will always remember about this beautiful young man was the complete love and admiration he had for his family. Throughout all he went through, his thoughts were on his family and how he had caused them distress. He was worried about them, not his own wellbeing.

Each time I look at the ocean I will remember this young man and how much love he created. What a beautiful legacy to leave behind for the world.

As we go through life, we don't always say how we feel to the people we love. We all know death is inevitable, but unless we are undergoing illness we often think we have time. These feelings are usually known by our loved ones but aren't always voiced aloud. We think they can be said at a later date. But death can be unpredictable. Even those of us with the ability to see in the future aren't always given knowledge on a death that is to come.

A sudden death leaves a strong imprint on your mind and heart. It strongly brings forward the last moments you spent with your loved one who is now physically gone forever. You will replay those moments many times. Hopefully, within those precious moments, you will remember shared words of love between you.

But whether you have shared these loving words or not, I can tell you from that day forward you will be more focused on telling people in your life how very much they are loved and appreciated.

Don't wait until you think the time is right. There doesn't need to be a 'right' time to tell those that are special to you they are loved. Sit down and have conversations with those you care for. Tell them moments when they made you laugh or feel loved. Tell them how they encouraged you and made you feel special. Tell them truths you have held in your mind and not voiced, even if those truths are difficult to voice. Leave no words unsaid.

I have had many clients say to me, 'Can you please tell my loved one I love them?' And of course I will do this, but I let the client know their loved one in spirit hears every word they say. I also know if my client had a wish, they would wish to say it to their loved one in person and hear those same words returned.

Life is fleeting. Hug those you love. Tell people how much they are loved and appreciated, each time you see them. Because one day you will remember the last moment you spent with them and know you can never return to that moment ever again. So, make it a moment you will always treasure.

Chapter Nine

LIFE DECLINED

My mind is so tired and weary.
No peace seems to enter.
Life holds no joy or motivation, all seems so dreary.

All the time my mind seems to be screaming.
I can't make it stop, all these words pounding in my head.
No time for rest, all it focuses on is negativity and scheming.

Deep within I know people care, I know I am loved.
But these screaming words in my head wash all that away.
All I feel is lost and alone. They shout I'm a burden,
no good and unloved.

Life is hard, each day takes so much energy.
There are people I know who wonder and care.
But I've learned to hide my feelings, my thoughts,
my painful days so expertly.

I know deep within you care and love me dearly.
But the blackness of my sick mind seems to have so much power.
I've let you down, but I cannot see a way to stay. I apologise sincerely.

Life is hard, my mind is unwell and life seems so unkind.
Please help me, reach out, show me a way, I'm losing my battle.
It seems life I have declined.

I see no way out, no way to find the strength to live another day.
I'm hurting in so many ways I don't show. Why do I feel so numb?
Please remember me in better days.
Those days when my mind was well. This I wish and pray.

I thought long and hard about whether I should put this chapter in my book. But I heard my guides say, 'Little One, this is important and it should be included.'

Death by suicide is one of the hardest deaths to come to terms with. It leaves so many unanswered questions and deep grief. My own family has experienced a death by suicide and I have seen the devastating effects it can cause to those left behind.

I remember many years ago, reading for a young blonde man in a shop I worked in. Unfortunately, this gentleman had decided he would end his own life. To him, it seemed easier than having to deal with the harshness of life and a mind that was unwell.

I patiently tried to explain to him how devastated his mother, family and friends would feel if he ended his life in this way.

He nodded and replied, 'They will be better off without me in the long term.'

He then proceeded to tell me that all would be okay when he entered the afterlife. He would be well and happy, and that his family should be happy for him that he's no longer in pain. I explained that I understood what he was saying, and yes, there is no pain in the afterlife. But he would have to look at how his actions affected those he left behind and that would be extremely hard to do. Spirit would ask him to undertake a lot of lessons and there would be a lot of hard work to heal his spirit.

I spent a long time with this young man, talking about his views on the afterlife and suicide. I spent well over an hour trying to persuade him to agree to me getting him some help. At one point I had the owner of the shop knocking on my door asking if all was okay.

Eventually, I had to let him leave my room as I had clients waiting. But as I walked him out, I knew he would not be on this earth for long and there was nothing I could do about it.

I woke up a week later to the song, 'Suicide Blonde' and instantly knew he had taken his life. A few weeks later I spoke to his dear mum. I explained that he just wouldn't budge on his notion of life being better if he wasn't here and saw suicide as the only option.

I have done many suicide readings in my time and they can be very emotional for my client. I will often hear, 'But why didn't they love me enough to stay, to keep trying?' Unfortunately, mental illness is just not that simple. In my visions I often see the person seems to be almost on automatic pilot. They don't think the act they are about to commit is the most final thing they will ever do and there is not return. This often seems strange to me. How can you not realise when you put a gun to your head or a noose around your neck that this will be your final act on this earth? But often this is the case. People in such turmoil and mental anguish are just not thinking clearly. They often do not seem to fully comprehend the consequences of their actions.

I remember reading for a beautiful mother who lost her son to suicide at a very young age. He had been given a drug by a doctor for another complaint and soon after taking this medication his whole demeanour and personality seemed to change. He went from a bright, happy young boy, to someone who was in the depths of despair and focused on killing himself. His mother constantly voiced her fears to the doctor, explaining her son had changed once being put on this drug. But the doctor didn't listen to her pleas to look further into the drug he had prescribed. Unfortunately, her beautiful boy committed suicide and the drug was later found to be the catalyst for why. The drug was eventually evaluated by the medical profession and they found it did indeed cause these negative side effects.

It breaks my heart when I read for a mother who has lost her child to suicide. Whether they're eight or forty-eight, I feel the grief of a mother who will never fully recover from their beloved child's death.

There are times I read for people who think their loved ones have committed suicide, only to find by talking to the person in spirit and seeing what happened through the visions, that suicide was not the cause of death. Their death was accidental.

I remember reading for a client who thought her relative had committed suicide. As I began talking to the young man in spirit, I knew by what he was saying and showing me that it was a complete accident.

He had been walking home after a night out and was a little worse for wear after consuming a lot of alcohol. He was annoyed that his night had finished badly due to an argument, but he definitely didn't have suicide on his mind.

He was walking along a road and a truck was coming up behind him. Looking over his shoulder as the truck was nearing him, he stumbled, causing his body to fall into its path. The truck killed him instantly. This man had not intentionally taken his life. But as in any small town, the rumours had started and people drew their own conclusions to why he died that night. These conclusions were wrong.

Death can occur in many different ways. Each death will impact the ones we love in its own unique way. It often brings questions to the fore that can go unanswered.

I have been reading for a beautiful family for a number of years. I first read for them many years ago when I lived in my hometown. I knew the young woman that sat before me but had no prior knowledge of her family history. The wonderful thing about reading for people, is at times they often become my meditation students. And some even become my dearest friends.

Starting the reading, I could see there were many people in spirit wishing to step forward for this beautiful lady who sat before me. But one female was almost demanding to be the first to speak. As the reading progressed, I realised it was her sibling.

It is a medium's job to prove the person lives on in spirit. The term for this is 'proof of survival.' We must show we know details about the person in spirit so there is no doubt they still live on in spirit. Some of these details may be concerning what is going on in the family or physical attributes of the person.

Due to the fact I don't always remember what I say in a reading, I asked this client many years later what I said that made her know without a doubt I was communicating with her sister. She explained I had given her in-depth information on the family and my mannerisms when talking to her were the same as her sister's. There was one feature of her sister I would never have known, and that was her beautiful, long curled hair. I had described it like Julia Roberts in the movie *Pretty Woman*, only darker.

Intuitively, my client had felt something was wrong and had been ringing her sister but there was no answer. She knew that her sister needed to be checked on. Listening to the sister's concerns and her intuitive feelings, the family did do a welfare check and found the sister dead. I have no doubt her sister in spirit had been around her, trying to get a message to my client regarding her passing.

As the months and years progressed, I had the privilege of reading for this young woman's other sister and brother. They are a large family and their bonds are very strong.

The first sister had passed my details onto her younger sister, and as she came into the room I felt their sister in spirit come forward. My client had only given her first name to me. In those days, I didn't actually take a last name when booking my clients in for a reading.

The woman in spirit came forward and spoke to me, saying, 'This is my sister,' and shortened her name as she did when she was living. I called her by the name given to me by her sister in spirit and told her I knew they were sisters. The sister in spirit mentioned they were alike, but added, 'Only the good bits though' with a bit of a chuckle. All this happened before my client had even sat down.

The woman in spirit was vivacious and beautiful. She was straight to the point and very anal in how she organised herself in life, but I could feel she also struggled with life in some ways. I loved the way she delivered her messages, and still do. We seemed to hit it off straight away. I guess in a lot of ways we were similar.

She began to show me her passing. I could see she was weary and was getting ready to get into bed. I knew she had had some prescription medication but for some reason it looked like she was having more. Her head was fuzzy and she seemed confused. I wondered why she had taken more, but I knew this was not an intentional act of having had enough and wanting to end her life.

I asked her, mind to mind, why she took more medication?

Her reply was, 'I didn't realise I had taken the first lot and by the time I had swallowed the second lot, it was too late.'

I then saw her in her bed feeling extremely dazed, followed by the realisation something was dramatically wrong. She could see the room around her, aware of her surroundings but unable to move her body, no matter how hard she tried. Then, she just seemed to drift off into unconsciousness. Before long, she was gone.

This was not a suicide. I knew this with every fibre of my being.

The woman in spirit agreed, saying, 'I didn't mean to do it, I was so exhausted I had forgotten I had taken the first lot.'

Her death was caused by an overdose of prescription drugs. It was an accidental overdose. This beautiful young woman had lost her life due to a simple, yet tragic, mistake. Her family would now have to deal with the fact that she would never return to the physical world.

Down the track, I also read for her brother. Even though he looked extremely different from his sisters, I knew immediately they were related. I told him I knew who he was and his sister in spirit was coming forward for him.

I remember the sister in spirit saying, 'He needs help to deal with my death. He was the one who found me. He thinks he could have got to me sooner and holds guilt.' I said this gently to the young man and could see he was getting emotional.

'There was nothing you could have done,' I said, explaining I knew he was the one who had found her. The man was a paramedic and no doubt had been instrumental in helping a lot of people over his career. But sadly, fate had decided he couldn't save his own sister.

The thing I find so wonderful about the sister in spirit, is she always uses her words to create laughter. Basically, she says it how it is! He laughed when she said he wasn't as soft as the first sister I had read for and wasn't as hard as the second sister. I also laughed knowing exactly what she meant having read for both women.

Their spirit sister always brings through lots of information clairvoyantly about the family when I read for her siblings. From pinpointing problems with family and relationships, to change of careers and family celebrations. She even showed me when her brother was contemplating writing a book and gave him advice on publishing.

I know she is pleased her sister and I have formed a very special bond that will never be broken. Although I still kind of roll my eyes and laugh when she calls me The Wizard! But I do know the term is always said with love and respect.

I still use a gift she sent me which had a photo of myself wearing a wizard hat on it! It made me laugh hysterically when I first laid eyes on it. The image has now faded after regular use, but each time I pick it up I smile, remembering a gift sent with love.

Why did I write of the sister in spirit in this chapter? Her death definitely wasn't a suicide. I placed her in this chapter because even though a coroner's report may say death by accidental overdose, this type of death can still make people question things when there is no need. Unfortunately, tragedies happen. That is just a part of life. But I can say one thing. Her family know without a doubt that their loving sister hadn't taken her own life.

There are so many reasons why a person feels they can no longer live on this earth. Yes, mental illness is often a major reason. But there are also times when a person may feel it is their choice and would be a better option for themselves and their loved ones. This may happen when a person is diagnosed with a terminal illness and has decided to leave on their own terms. In their minds, they think it is better for all concerned. They don't want to put themselves or their loved ones through the pain of watching them go through a long and drawn out illness, and then ultimately death. These people don't have mental illness, they just have made the choice to leave this world when the body dictates it is time. And I understand this completely.

I remember talking to a dear older lady who was in her nineties. She had been diagnosed with breast cancer and her family wanted her to go through the arduous rounds of chemotherapy. She came into my room and we started talking about what was going on with her. I knew she really didn't want to go through this process, and at her age she was ready to pass into the world of spirit. No, she hadn't given up on life. She had had a good life living into her nineties, but now she was tired and felt she had done enough.

As we progressed with the reading, I said to her, 'You know, it's okay if you want to say no to the treatment, don't you?'

She bowed her head and said, 'They expect me to, Trina.'

I assured her that her family loved her dearly and they just wanted to have her with them as long as they could. But it was also okay if she didn't want to proceed. The next day, she told her family of her decision, and of course they supported her in that decision. Was her decision suicide? No, of course not. She just wanted to do what her body would naturally do in its own time. I've written about her because it is important we understand we all have free will and choices to make, each and every day of our lives.

No matter what life deals you, you always have the ultimate decision in how you react to those hardships. Free will is always involved. Each decision you make in your life will be based on free will. Those choices you make will then create a scenario of events. Yes, we have been given a physical body, but within that body lives your soul. You come to this earth to learn many lessons. Those lessons are given to you to advance the learning of your soul.

Be assured, those that have chosen to take their lives by suicide are always greeted with love when they pass to the world of spirit. No, they are not shunned and sent to a deep dark place, never to be seen again. There are no harsh judgements made by those in spirit about the action they have taken. Like all souls, they are shown how their actions on Earth have affected those they love. And yes, they are shown things that will be very difficult to deal with. But through time spent with wise souls in spirit, they will always have the opportunity to heal. They will ultimately be embraced by the light of spirit. Remember, the world of spirit is based on love, not punishment!

There are so many lessons a death can teach us. Each person who is impacted by death will have their own unique lessons to learn. Suicide teaches us an important lesson, in that it asks us to be mindful of the people who come into our lives. It teaches us about the masks people often wear. Masks that hide their turmoil or who they truly are deep down. It asks us to be compassionate to those we live with and understand we are all unique. Our different life experiences can sometimes send us into turmoil. Those we love can be in pain and we may have no idea of the depth of that pain ... We must take the time to care for each other and connect at a deeper level. We must let go of judgement and use compassion and empathy instead. Because that's what our world needs at the moment. That's a soul lesson that each one of us who walks this earth should be open to learning, each and every day we live.

And please remember, no matter whether the death is suicide, accidental or even the refusing of medical treatment, spirit will always be there to greet these souls and embrace them with love.

Chapter Ten

ANIMAL FRIENDS

I come to you for a reason, to show you a very special love.
We will have a bond like no other.
Somehow, I know I have been sent to you from above.

My body may be covered in fur, feathers or even scales.
My world is so different from yours.
But oh, how our friendship will create so many wonderful tales.

I feel your touch and how you lovingly hold me close.
Two hearts joining together in love.
You see me as your friend and I will be there for
all your highs and lows.

Each day you will greet me as though I am one of the family.
And I will look to you for nourishment and shelter.
But most of all, I will embrace your world with
my own kind of rhapsody.

My whole world will revolve around you.
My master, my carer, my companion, my best friend.
And I know in my heart, you love me as I do you.

Always remember I am by your side, your loyal friend.
Even when my life here on Earth ceases to exist.
And I will be lovingly watching over you until we meet again.

I have had the pleasure of reading many animals over my time. It's always a little bit of a weird experience for myself, as I often become the animal to feel any of their physical problems. Yep, even I find that a little strange!

'What did you do at work today, Trina?'

'Oh, nothing much, I just became a dog!' What?!

Yes, I actually feel myself becoming the animal so that I may pinpoint where any physical problems are present within their body. I have done readings on dogs, cats, farm animals, horses, greyhounds and race horses, even the odd rabbit. I often have people bring in photographs of animals that are trained to race or are in the equestrian area. I find these readings very interesting. I actually had a man name his racing greyhound after myself. He named it, 'Trina's Spirit.' I have no idea if it won any races, as seriously I have no interest whatsoever in gambling.

Animals can teach us so many things about life. I think the most important lesson they will ever teach you, is unconditional love. Our beloved pets give us so much joy. They often teach us to slow down and see what truly is important in our lives. The moment we become a pet owner, we begin to understand how important it is to be responsible for someone other than ourselves. We become aware that they depend on us for their wellbeing. This bond also teaches us to have empathy. I think that is very much needed in our world.

How relaxing is it to curl up with a cat and feel and listen to their gentle purr? Or to be greeted by a beloved dog, so excited to see you that not only their tail is wagging with joy? Their whole body seems to physically change filling with joy and showing you that you are the best thing they have ever seen. Even if they have seen you only an hour before.

I'm sure each of us who have been pet owners have at some time told our animals our worries and concerns. That beloved animal will often look at you, with eyes that show they know you are having a difficult time and need them to be at your side. You feel their love so strongly and it feels as though they understand everything you are saying. They provide an energy of comfort.

Like us humans, each animal has their own personality. They have their own fears, idiosyncrasies and life experiences. And yes, even bad habits! Some animals will want lots of physical contact and others would prefer you stay your distance until they decide to come closer. Others are serious, even a bit neurotic, while others act as the class clown. All traits us humans have! But unlike us, animals often forgive so much more easily.

There are many times a beloved pet will come through in a reading to show their owner they are watching over them from spirit. Animals, like children in spirit, show me the most beautiful images of where they are in the world of spirit. I love seeing an old animal show me how spritely they are, now they have shed their earthly body.

Often, the animal talks of their owner's very difficult decision to euthanise them and how they appreciated their decision even though it was so hard for them to make. It certainly is a difficult decision, but I think, to release an animal from a life of physical pain is the ultimate act of love given by its owner. This act shows the depth of love that person has for their furry friend. They know full well they will miss them dearly and grieve deeply their loss for a very long time. They put the wellbeing of the animal before their own needs. To me, that is a very special gift of love.

I remember a dear friend texting me one day. His beloved cat was very ill and he had to have him euthanised. This gorgeous fluff ball with brilliant, intense eyes had brought such joy into my friend's life. His beautiful companion had kidney issues. Even though they had only been together for a short time, I could feel his sorrow.

This man, who is extremely spiritual and has the kindest sensitive heart, knew without a doubt his fur friend would be greeted by his family in spirit and embraced in love. But I felt his pain at the realisation he would no longer be physically in his arms. I assured him the cat would be looked after and I would send my guide Oringo to be with him as he passed into the world of spirit.

Some hours later I received the most beautiful, yet heartbreaking video of my friend saying goodbye to his little fur friend. My heart felt the beautiful bond of love between them and also the pain of having to say a final goodbye.

Oringo stepped forward and asked me to relay a message to my friend.

He said, 'Your feline friend is with loved ones in spirit and resting well. He will visit you often and thanks you for your kindness and love. Now, grieve a love that was unconditional and know you were given this animal for a reason.'

I do believe we are given animals for a reason and that they are there to teach us many different soul lessons.

I asked my friend at a later date what he thought his fur friend had taught him. He had initially brought him into his life as a therapy animal, to help him unwind from mental stress caused by his very busy businesses, and also, to deal with a toxic business mentor that made my friend's self-esteem plummet. His beautiful little fluff ball had also helped him immensely when Covid struck.

Once his cat had passed on to the world of spirit, he used the love he had for his cat to create a legacy. He wanted his cat's life to mean something.

For the first time in seven years, this gentleman stood up to his toxic mentor and said, 'ENOUGH! You are no longer welcome in my life. I'm smart, I know I am capable and I'm loved by many.'

For the first time he was able to stand his ground and own his power. He knew this man must no longer be in his life. This little bundle of fur had taught him how important it is to only have people in his life that supported him in a positive way along his path.

I'm sure he will hold many beautiful memories of his feline friend within his heart, and smile each time these come into his mind.

I will always remember this man's act of unconditional love. Letting a beloved fur friend go to the world of spirit, knowing he would no longer be in pain. To me, that is the ultimate act of love as a pet owner.

Animals grieve too! I remember many years ago living next door to a family. Their dog never really made much noise at all. He didn't bark unless someone was going into his yard. Even then, it was more about letting his owner know there was someone coming, rather than wanting to attack. The father, I must admit, was a bit of a grumpy man. He never really spoke much more than a gruff 'Hello.' But he always spent time with the dog and I knew they had a close bond. Unfortunately, the father died quickly and unexpectedly. For the next few days, the dog howled constantly. It was a howl that was so mournful and sad. My mother commented on this and I remember Dad saying he must be missing his owner and I nodded in agreement. Yes, I could feel the depth of his sorrow each time I heard him howl and I felt his pain as I listened at the fence as he whimpered. Whenever there is deep love there will always be deep grief, whether you are a human or an animal.

I have also had experiences where an animal in spirit will tell their beloved owner about the complexities of another animal they own. This is so the owner understands more deeply how they need to be looked after, and whether there are any negative traits, such as the potential to be aggressive or anxious. This type of information is very important and can show the owner what the animal needs to become an integral part of the family.

This is an act of love by the animal in spirit. But there are times when I hear from the animal in spirit that the living animal is definitely not as good as them as a pet. I laugh and say, 'I think someone may be a little biased!' when I relay the message. But you know what? Most times the owner actually agrees with the animal in spirit, which usually ends up in us both laughing.

Animals of all kinds pick up on the energy of Spirit. I've found over my years working as a clairvoyant medium I sometimes have to be more aware of how they react to my energy. Why? Because this Little One never goes anywhere on her own. I'm always surrounded by my guides in spirit and this can be a little bit disconcerting to an animal.

Many years ago, some close friends had come for dinner and brought their dog with them. I had seen and interacted with this dog many times prior to this night and he had never once reacted to me in a negative way. But that night, I had been asked some questions about Spirit and of course my guides came very close to me so I would give the appropriate answers. The night was ending and we went out on the porch. Immediately, the dog lurched towards me with teeth bared and barking furiously! We were completely taken aback.

Its owner apologised, saying, 'I don't know what's got into him.'

Luckily the dog had been chained to the Ute they had arrived in, otherwise I think this little clairvoyant would have ended up being the dog's dinner! But I understood he was reacting not to myself, but to all the people in spirit standing behind me. I always tend to give dogs plenty of time to adjust to how they feel my energy. To be quite honest, I guess everyone needs to have a little bit of time to get used to this little clairvoyant medium and the energy I bring! And I get that, I understand that!

I have had many pets over my time and always grieve their passing. Like any other pet owner, we have formed a very special bond. I have owned some beautiful dogs, my favourite being my Lassie dog. She often visits me in spirit, especially when I'm unwell. I have also tended to love the energy of cats and birds. Both are more open to dealing with the army of spirit people that surround me in my daily life. Cats have this innate ability to pick up spirits and not necessarily be freaked out by their presence. I have one cat, BJ, that often visits. He loves to jump up on my bed and lay with me when I'm watching a movie. All of my birds have been wild birds that come to me because they trust I would never hurt them in any way. Or they come because they are messengers from Spirit. We just have a unique connection and I have no doubt they will always be in my life. I think I will always be known as the birdwoman. Some, my neighbours especially, may even call me the crazy birdwoman. And yep, even I would agree with that.

Another animal that comes to visit me is my blue dog. I explained earlier how he came to visit me as a child. Although he's not technically a dog, because he's actually a wolf. But I still call him My Blue Dog.

These days, My Blue Dog only comes to me to soften the emotional blow of My Indian leaving, or to comfort me on an emotional level. The last time I saw My Blue Dog was when My Indian had to leave after working with me on a silent retreat. As I was meditating, a song I had not chosen came on my playlist. It was called 'Metamorphosis.' My Indian came forward and everything disappeared as he showed me this song in visions. It was the most beautiful thing I had ever seen, but I knew he was showing me it was time for him to leave again. The tears began to flow down my cheeks and I could feel his love surround me with such strength. I watched as the words and his visions came together in such a powerful, yet beautiful way. I didn't want to open my eyes because I knew once I did, he would be gone.

'Little One, you must open your eyes. It is time.' But the tears continued and I refused. I didn't want him to go. He then showed me the Blue Dog. 'Little One, I will leave the dog with you. Just as he did when you were a child, he will comfort you and be at your side until you are ready to let go. When you need him he will return to your side. Now open your eyes and remember I love you. I am always but a breath away. Remember this to be true, my stubborn Little One.'

Reluctantly I opened my eyes and sobbed, grieving for My Indian, not knowing when I would see him again. My Blue Dog came very close and put his head in my lap as I sobbed and I hugged him tightly knowing he was a gift of love from a teacher and friend I love deeply. My Blue Dog stayed with me for many weeks, until finally I felt his energy gently disappear. But as I write this and feel the emotion of remembering such a beautiful experience, he sits at my side gently nuzzling my leg. He is letting me know he feels my loss and is here to comfort me. I know when My Indian can't be by my side My Blue Dog will always come to me when I need comfort. And I know I'm truly blessed and loved.

My meditation classes often involve the topic of animals. The animals we have loved in spirit have the ability to return and watch over us, as they did when they were on Earth. I also teach about animal guides and how animals can teach us lessons as we go through our daily lives.

An animal can show up in your life to signal a teaching your soul wants you to learn. For instance, you may keep seeing a butterfly, or find butterflies come into your life through the media, books or even in your daily conversations.

So, what can a butterfly teach us?

A butterfly goes through transformation. They go from egg to larvae to pupa and finally become the beautiful butterfly with gossamer wings we admire. Throughout our own lives, we need to transform from one state of self to another. We transform as we evolve in our thinking and ways of perceiving the world around us. The butterfly can teach us it's time to grow out of the old self and develop into a new form of ourselves. The butterfly has a natural lightness to its energy and often asks us to rise above all that may be weighing us down.

Every animal can teach us humans a thing or two. But first, we must watch their behaviour and how they interact with the world, in order to completely understand the lessons they bring. Often people talk of having a loved one in spirit who had an affinity with an animal, bird or insect. That animal may appear in ways that show them their loved one in spirit is near. That, I can definitely vouch for and assure you is a common way for those in spirit to connect with you.

Those of us who have had the privilege of owning a pet will be given many lessons to learn. Patience, responsibility, empathy, trust, fun, strength. The list is endless. But I think the most important lesson they teach us, is unconditional love.

Chapter Eleven

THIS IS ME

I came to this earth in search of myself.
Maybe a story to tell when I grow old and weary.
At times my journey seemed to be to prove oneself.

But I do not dwell just in one world, this earth.
I travel between two worlds, this one and the next.
The world of spirit showing me the mysteries of rebirth.

Visions, voices and feelings show proof of great love.
Of times on this earth now shared from those passed.
Spirit now watching over us all from above.

At times there is confusion, what is it you show?
What of these images, songs and sayings, what do they all mean?
Times when I shake my head and do not know.

Yet in those times when the messages are so clear,
I know with undeniable faith,
Why Spirit works through me and why I am here.

There are often times when I have no idea what a person in spirit is trying to convey to their loved one. No matter how hard I try, I cannot understand what they wish to pass on. There are also times when I cannot reach the person in spirit that my client wants to speak to. I always state I cannot promise to bring a specific loved one in on the day of my client's reading. No medium can promise this. I often say if I could click my fingers and have someone in spirit just appear, I'd probably be talking to someone famous like Elvis Presley or Princess Diana all day. But I can't. It's probably just as well, because I could imagine spending most of my time talking to famous dead people and getting nothing done all day.

The last couple of chapters I have concentrated on my mediumship. A medium is someone who shows that life goes on after death of the physical body. But there are times in my readings when the focus is more on my clairvoyant abilities. All mediums are psychic, not all psychics are mediums. But please do understand, not all mediums focus on clairvoyance in their readings. Clairvoyant readings are about giving guidance on what is to come in the future. In most of my readings I use both abilities, but if I see my client needs mostly direction for the future then this is what I will concentrate on. My work will always be focused on what my client needs in order to help them create a better life.

When I work clairvoyantly, I use a number of senses and call on different guides to help me with the guidance needed for my client. Claire is always standing with me when I work and is very good at helping me in any way I need.

If I'm doing a medical intuitive reading, I will call on My Doctor in spirit. He helps me get to the core of the problem and what is to happen in the future.

My Doctor has been with me for many years. I remember when he first came in while I was doing a healing on a client. He stepped forward and gave me the mental image of the person's body being opened, so I could see how the organs worked inside the body. And I admit that was a bit of a shock to my eyes and I wasn't quite sure why it was necessary until he explained the reasons. This was done so I had some idea of how the body worked and how different organs could be affected when illness occurred. He thought it was important I saw the mechanics of the human body so I could understand when something was wrong and illness was present within the body.

Now please understand I'm not a doctor and I won't ever say to take my advice over your own doctor's. But My Doctor in spirit is extremely good at diagnosing and trying to help rectify physical problems within a client.

Many years ago, I read for an older gentleman. He was old school and like most men, he didn't frequent the doctor as often as he should. He hadn't come to me for a medical reading, in fact, it was my mediumship skill he was seeking. He was a lovely man who actually reminded me a great deal of my own father in spirit.

But My Doctor stepped forward, saying it was important the man seek medical advice promptly. I could see there was something wrong with his heart. My Doctor showed me if this problem wasn't rectified within a couple of weeks he would die. Of course, I didn't say this to my client as I didn't want him to freak out.

I told him, 'My guides are saying you need to seek medical advice on your heart, there is something wrong.'

All he said was, 'Oh, okay.'

My Doctor whispered in my ear to be more persistent. I wasn't to let him go without him promising he would visit the doctor within the week. I talked to him about losing my own father at forty-five to a heart attack and how devastated I was and still was.

He shook his head and said, 'That's very sad, Trina, to lose your dad so young.'

I replied, 'Think about how your family would feel if you were no longer here.'

I spent two hours with this gentleman, trying to get him to promise me he would visit the doctor. Eventually, he agreed to make an appointment that week.

Me being who I am, a very stubborn woman, said, 'Okay, wonderful. Now shake on it!'

He looked at me a bit sheepishly, but then shook my hand saying, 'Okay, okay. You're a very stubborn woman, Trina.'

I knew he was old school, and if I got a handshake then he would actually make that appointment.

A week later he called me. His specialist had told him to ring me and say thank you, because if he hadn't taken my advice he would be dead. He had a major undiagnosed heart problem and was to go into surgery the following week.

I said, 'See, I do know what I'm talking about and I'm very glad you took my advice. I knew you wouldn't have gone if you hadn't shaken my hand.'

We both laughed and he agreed, saying, 'You're a sneaky little one, aren't you? But thank you.'

He was fine after his operation and continued to enjoy good health from that day forward.

Unfortunately, there have been times I have read for people, only to find out they had died shortly after. My guides hadn't warned of their imminent death.

When I have asked why, their reply is, 'Little One, you are not always given all the information. This is the way of Spirit. If a soul is to leave your world then it will be so. Your abilities cannot change this fact. It is not necessary for you to relay the information as this is their path and cannot be changed.'

One of my favourite ways to read for a client is when they bring in a photograph. I especially like reading photographs of a children. But I only take photographs of living people. It's my job as a medium to describe the dead physically when reading for them. This is usually done in a collaboratory way using the person's relatives in spirit and my own guides.

People think you can tell a lot by a photograph, but I'm trained not to focus on the image in the photo. I focus on the energy of the person. I'm also not allowed to wear my glasses in a reading, so most times I can't actually see the image portrayed in the photograph. Photographs can lie, they don't always show the core of the person. I'll put my hand on it for a few seconds, until I have a flow of words moving through my mind. If a photo isn't available, I can usually still read that person by focusing on their name.

I love seeing children grow, whether they are in the womb, a week old, a toddler or teenager. I love to see their personality traits and idiosyncrasies develop before my eyes. With the help of My People in spirit we can often see where the parent can overcome obstacles. Things like control issues, anxiety or health issues the child may have in the future. If the child is within the womb we can help the mother better prepare for the birth and point out any issues that may come up. We also give advice on how to deal with the child as they grow, such as if they are going to feed well or sleep well.

Each child is a unique individual. We can often see if they are sensitive and hold great empathy. We look at if they will find the world difficult to deal with, and how to aid both parent and child to cope with what is to come in the future. I love seeing how different children engage with their parents. And often I advise the parent how their child is using their sensitivity. This might be to avoid certain things, like going out of their comfort zone, or they may be actually taking advantage of the parent in some way – this happens a lot!

I've done readings on three of my grandchildren. I did this when they were a few weeks old, to give their parents some idea of what they needed to prepare for. All of my grandchildren are gorgeous, loving, unique little individuals and I have no doubt they will keep their parents on their toes in the future.

Can a photograph reading be done on anyone and anything? Yes, unless I hear 'ethics' from my guides. This usually means the person who has brought me the photograph has no right to the information. The person could be acting in an unethical way, wanting to hurt the person in the photo. Or, it may mean they are just being a busy body who really shouldn't be privy to the information. Over my time as a reader, I have read for all types of people, animals, houses and businesses in photographs. I find all of these interesting to read.

As I said earlier, I don't take photographs of those who are deceased, but on the odd occasion I have done so. Usually it's done to find out details of ancestry like a family tree. Or, it could be to explain the reason someone died and why that death occurred.

Sometimes the details in my readings are quite specific and other times they may not make sense to myself or the client. I'm often given words or information and have no idea what they actually mean. Spirit uses what I have within my brain and my level of experience to relay the information. I may be shown a film like *The Sound of Music* and that will pinpoint where I am with regards to location. Or, I may be shown the human body and how it works and then why the client's body isn't working well. Remember I'm not a doctor and I definitely haven't travelled to all the corners of our world. They have to use what I have experienced in my brain, then they take it to another level. What do I mean by that? I don't know everything, but by using what I know and adding in things I don't know (through images, words, taste and feelings), it becomes similar to putting a jigsaw puzzle together. And soon I have a full picture of what's happening.

People often ask me how I deal with being who I am and what I do. Well, the answer to that is I can't be anyone other than who I am. I also really haven't known any difference because I grew up with my abilities. However, I have brought in a few things that help me as I walk my path. One of these is what I call an 'on and off' switch. When I'm working I have my 'on' switch turned on. That means I'm open to talking to the people in spirit and looking into the future. When I turn the switch to 'off' I'm pretty much just going about my life as anyone else does. Now, I may need to clarify. I don't have these buttons physically placed anywhere on my body. I do admit I can be a little bit weird – but not that much of a weirdo! It's actually a mental intention. Having said all that, I still get clairvoyant things coming through, no matter if I'm switched on or off! It's just who I am. It does mean though I don't get bombarded by every Tom, Dick and Harry in spirit as I walk down the street or as I do my grocery shopping.

When I was growing up, the dead people would often just appear in front of me and that actually used to startle me. Imagine turning around in your bedroom and seeing a man you don't know standing there looking at you. Yep, that's going to make anyone's heart rate quicken. You see, in those days when the dead people came forward, I would see them exactly like I see a living person. It took me a few seconds to realise they were actually in spirit. As I grew and matured, I made it a rule that all people who are now in spirit must come through my ear first. They couldn't just pop in unannounced. In other words, I would be warned by words in my mind or I would see an image of the person in my mind first. Those two things informed me that someone wished to converse with me. It was a much more civilised and calm way of dealing with all those who wished to pass on messages from spirit.

I actually find the living people I come into contact with each day more of a problem than any dead person I have had to contend with. Living people tend to have a trove of emotions that come with their energy. Anger, anxiety, depression, fear and jealousy, just to name a few. All these emotions can impact my own energy quite strongly and if I'm not careful, it can affect me in a negative way, both mentally and physically. Doing a protection for my energy and having that on/off button in play helps me cope day to day. If at any stage my guides in spirit think I'm being negatively affected they will step forward, gently placing their hand on my head to remind me to check in with my own energy.

I absolutely love doing this work, joining forces with my guides and those in spirit. To be quite honest, I really can't see myself doing any other type of work these days. In the past I have had other occupations, but none really gave me the satisfaction like my work with Spirit. However, the downside is this work can take a toll on myself – emotionally, mentally and physically.

Some people might see me sitting in front of them and think it's only an hour's work, that it's not going to make me tired. Most days that is the case and I walk away feeling uplifted and satisfied. What people don't understand, is there is a lot of mental concentration that goes into a reading and that can be mentally draining. During a reading I also use my physical body a lot. Yep, I can hear your brains ticking over as you read that last statement. 'What does she mean? I don't see her physically doing a lot!'

When I was younger, I would often twitch as I was reading. The left side of my face would automatically start twitching as Spirit came closer. My arm would move as well. This did cause a few problems at times, as I was born with a problem with my neck. The twitching would often put my neck out if I had a large tic and that caused a painful reaction that could last for days. I learned after quite a few years, that if I scribbled on paper as I read, I didn't twitch. So unfortunately, I've probably been the cause of quite a few trees being cut down from our earth. But scribbling is a necessary thing these days so my body doesn't seize up!

I also physically feel what my client feels, especially if they have an illness. So, I want you to imagine how your body would feel at the end of the day if it had to constantly feel the pain of a bad hip or knee, even though that pain didn't belong to you. Of course, I am in control of what level of discomfort I allow myself to feel. The discomfort will leave the instant I have finished my reading, but it can be wearing on the body.

To do a reading, it is also necessary to raise my energy so I may connect with those in spirit. Again, this means I use my own physical energy to some extent.

The emotional area is probably the easiest for me to deal with. I have always been taught to emotionally detach from what I see, hear and experience in a reading. Because of this detachment, I don't actually remember a great deal of the contents of my readings, or in fact my clients!

When commencing a reading, I ask my clients if they have been with me before as often I won't remember that they have. Once, I remember returning to Victoria and visiting a psychic fair one of my friends was working at. A lady approached me with a big smile on her face. She grabbed my arm and began talking to me.

'Trine, it's so good to see you. Are you reading here today?'

I thought to myself, well I must know her because she called me Trine not Trina! But for the life of me I seriously didn't know who she was. She apologised when she saw my look of confusion. I definitely haven't got a poker face! She then explained I had done a number of readings for her in the past and thanked me for my guidance.

She ended the conversation with, 'It's okay, I knew you wouldn't remember me. You always said in each reading you don't retain anything once you have finished the reading. I just wanted to say hello.'

Often people come up to me saying, 'I know you won't remember me, but I'm so and so.' They then continue to re-introduce themselves and tell me why they have approached me.

Again, I hear your mind ticking over, wondering how I wrote about the people in this book? The answer to that, is the readings I have included in my book are clients I have seen a number of times. Their readings touched my heart in a way I just couldn't forget. Having said that, a few of these beautiful people also sent me descriptions of some of the experiences they had when I read for them. This helped immensely when writing their stories.

Would I have liked to have included other stories from clients? Yes, of course. But I also have always been very mindful of people's privacy and know it can be emotionally hard for them to go over their loss. Some of my clients have actually said it isn't always the details they receive that assures them I am talking with their loved ones, it's the mannerisms and way I deliver their messages.

There are times when I'm describing a person in spirit and a client will say, 'Oh yes, that's so and so.' I'll then look over at the person in spirit to get the okay that it's actually them and the answer is no! Would it be easy for me to just say yes that's who it is? Most certainly! But I can tell you now, that's not going to happen. I'm extremely respectful of the work I do. Knowing that there are a lot of people out there doing this work that are downright dishonest and taking advantage of people really makes me angry. So, if the answer is 'no' to the identification of a person in spirit, the answer is no. I then have to gather more information so as the person I'm reading for can try to identify them.

Also, can I honestly say every reading I have done has been spot on? No, of course not! I'm human, I make mistakes just like everyone. And just like everyone in every industry I can have days that are better than others with regards to my work. Often, my guides in spirit will act as my manager and give me space with clients if I'm not feeling well or am too tired. On other occasions when I think I know best, I have been known to put clients in too late in the day or on days I wasn't supposed to be working.

When I do this, I look at my partner and say, 'I need to have a word with my manager or maybe even sack her.' He usually replies with a grin knowing full well I'm the one that mismanaged myself.

'Yep, she's getting out of hand and is a problem.'

On the whole, I try to balance my life as it should be. This will always entail work schedules that aren't too hectic and then adding rest and play. This act of balancing my lifestyle also involves some sort of silent retreat during the year, to gain greater insight into myself and to work with my guides in a more intense way.

My life is generally the same as everyone else's. It is filled with work, rest and play. I spend time doing the housework, running errands, talking to loved ones, arranging client appointments, exercising, listening to music, reading, writing and posting on my Facebook page. The only difference is I mix with the dead most days and enjoy our interactions immensely. My life really is the same as everyone else's, though. I'm juggling a number of things and hopefully living life to the fullest. But I'm always mindful of retaining balance in my life.

Chapter Twelve

LIFE IS FOR LAUGHTER

I have learned in life one must have laughter.
Working as a voice for those in spirit can be fun.
It does not mean all is serious in life or the hereafter.

We learn our lives must have a purpose.
Otherwise we walk along a tightrope,
Like an acrobat in a circus.

Lessons a plenty come into our lives.
Lessons we welcome and others we shun.
Some we master and others sit waiting in Spirit's archives.

Our minds grow and delve into why we are here,
Is there a simple answer?
Well, most will agree the answer is not always clear.

Faith in the workings of Spirit silence our fear.
Why does our mind question like it does?
Isn't it better to feel blessed we are still here?

So many lessons abound each and every day.
Patience, tolerance, belief in oneself.
These are just a few lessons that come our way.

But if we have belief in ourselves and see we are not perfect,
If we allow laughter and joy to touch our day,
We learn the energy of light will dive away all conflict.

Yes, be mindful of lessons that come your way,
But remember that each moment you live is precious,
And laughter must always be a part of your day.

I look back over my writing and must concede that it may look like my life is filled with lots of emotionally hard days. But please remember, these chapters have been lived over a number of years and I definitely have many days filled with joy and laughter. To be quite honest, my humour is often what keeps me going. Yes, life can be serious. But if we learn to see the humour even in our darkest days, it helps us to cope with life.

The work I do is often of a serious nature. How can it not be? On a daily basis I'm talking to people about their loved ones who now reside in spirit. There are times I sit across from a client in tears, but often mixed with those tears is laughter.

The people who come forward in spirit for my clients are often quite funny. The images they show me cracks me up with laughter.

I often have spirit people come forward saying 'Such and such needs to take their head out of where the sun don't shine.'

When I relay this type of message, my client usually nods their head in agreement and laughs.

There are so many sayings that are communicated by Spirit I'm supposed to pass on, and sometimes this can be quite funny. Often, they may hold a few swear words which I'm unable to include due to my grandmother in spirit who stands with me. She is always insistent I don't speak these words. So, I often ask for substitutes, but always relay to my client a swear word was used but I'm unable to say the word.

Usually I hear from the client, 'Yes, you can say it. I don't mind at all.'

Most often they will actually say, 'I bet it was this or that word.' And I of course will nod my head and chuckle.

Of course, over my time as reader I have become quite savvy at how to replace derogatory sayings or swear words and that becomes quite funny in itself. Often to my surprise, my grandmother in spirit will actually help me out with this. Which is again quite humorous to me. I remember one reading I was doing and the person in spirit was saying they needed to grow some balls. And just so you understand, I not only hear this term but I often get shown this in a literal way in my visions. Yes, I know the term means to man-up and respond maturely to a given situation or problem. But, I always want to try and keep the information relayed as close as possible to the way it was said by the person in spirit.

I could feel my grandmother come closer and knew immediately she would prefer me not to say the term. So, I'm thinking, *Well, how do I say that?* Please remember, I have this literal image of a man's genitals growing extremely large!

Through my ear I could hear her say in a quite matter of fact voice, 'Testicles!'

My client is often privy to the struggle I have with this type of sentence. And I'd say that's also a bit comical to witness. But yep, Gran was right. 'Testicles' is the correct term for balls.

So, I used the term and said, 'He needs to grow some testicles.'

I added that the term 'testicles' wasn't the actual word used by their loved one. Don't even think to ask me how I change the F-bomb into an appropriate word that my grandmother finds acceptable! But that's all part and parcel of what I do when I read for a client. Being flexible in how I do my readings has often been a great lesson to learn. And, it adds a bit of humour to what can otherwise be a very serious subject.

I often have people in spirit come forward and comment on their funerals. Readers, I need you to take notice of this. It's important to talk with your loved ones about what they want done when organising their funerals. I can tell you now, I have had a lot of spirit people shake their heads and roll their eyes when things haven't been done as they would have liked.

I really don't care what I'm buried in when my time comes. But there are a heck of a lot of women in spirit that come in saying, 'What in God's name were they thinking when they dressed me in that outfit?'

That statement is often cause for laughter. And, just for future reference, what your relatives dress you in for your funeral doesn't have to be what you are forced to wear forever in the afterlife.

I also hear those in spirit commenting on how they were portrayed as some angel, when obviously they weren't. They also comment why was so and so at their funeral when they could never be bothered with them when they were alive? Both are fair questions to ask, in my opinion.

I have given strict instructions to my family on what I would like at my own funeral. I've reminded them I'll come back to haunt them if they don't follow through with my instructions! My haunting would definitely include sitting on their bed, singing songs all through the night. Most of my family don't see my vocal prowess as being my greatest skill, so I'm pretty sure with that threat in mind they will make sure to adhere to my wishes!

Many times, when I am reading photographs of living children I will chuckle at the little antics they are get up to and what they are going to do in the future. When relaying that to my clients, they undoubtably end up laughing, nodding their head in agreement, even when these antics can be something they need to get advice on. It's funny to see in my visions a little poppet of three showing through their mannerisms how they can stand their own ground or enjoy the sound of music. Children have the uncanny gift of doing what comes naturally – and the poor parent has to deal with that!

But seriously, aren't they all such a joy? Writing that last sentence, I remember a maternal healthcare nurse saying that to me when one of my children had colic and wouldn't sleep.

I remember rolling my eyes as much as to say seriously I'm not seeing the joy at the moment. I laugh about that now, but I do remember and know how hard it is to be a parent. My advice? Cut yourself some slack. You're doing the best you can! Sit with the energy of your child and join in on their imagination and laughter. Doing this will allow your own energy to soar. Remember, your child absolutely loves to see you be childlike. So, get up and shake your butt to the music like a three-year-old and learn to let go of your inhibitions. Trust me, your child will remember those times and appreciate those wonderful memories in the future.

The people I deal with in spirit on a daily basis aren't always that serious. Even on the days I don't do readings, they often bring forward things that make me laugh. I remember the day I stumbled on the house we live in now. I had been doing a letterbox drop, advertising my meditation classes when we first arrived in Redcliffe. Coming up to this older style house, I saw three people looking at it. I thought to myself, I think this house is going to sale. The energy of the house was lovely and it was only a few metres from the water. I messaged my partner, saying I think this is the house we have been looking for.

Returning later that day, there was a 'For Sale' sign on the house and we immediately made a time to view the house. Walking inside, I was immediately drawn to the right of the room and saw an elderly lady in spirit wearing a long dress and apron. She looked around the door, poked her tongue out at me and then grinned. I knew immediately she came with the house and smiled to myself thinking, *I like this house.*

We bought the house that same day and love living here. I soon found out the room where I was to do my daily readings was occupied by the lady in spirit. I sat with her and discovered her name was Annie. She was very particular about making sure the house was secure. I thought it was a great thing, as we definitely wouldn't be getting intruders in this house.

We began renovating and were making great progress. At this stage, we didn't have roller doors to completely shut off the house from the outside world. So each day, I made sure that all the doors and windows were shut downstairs when I finished my work and I made my way up the stairs to our living area. Doing this would keep Annie happy.

One night I was in bed and Annie was at my side. She whispered, 'Luvvy, Luvvy, you need to go downstairs. It's not safe. The house is not safe.'

I sighed and got up.

Rusty, my partner, turned the light on and said, 'Sweetie, what are you doing?' I told him Annie said the house isn't safe. He chuckled and rolled over, knowing full well I had to check. On my return he asked, 'So was Annie, right?'

Yep. Apparently, I had left a window open just a little. Annie had watched me shut and lock the window and chuckled as I did so.

'Luvvy, remember I look after the house, now go to sleep.'

Annie always made sure nothing was left opened and often laughed when I questioned her. Especially when she knew I didn't want to get out of bed. A few months down the track, we had installed the roller doors and no one could get into our house without a great deal of effort.

But one night, Annie was again at my bedside. 'Luvvy, Luvvy, the house is not safe. You need to go downstairs.'

I rolled over and realised it was three in the morning. I really didn't want to get out of bed. So, I said to Annie, 'No, it's okay. It's all locked up.'

She persisted. 'Luvvy, get up and go downstairs.'

Life Is For Laughter

I threw off the bedcovers and walked down the stairs, grumpy about being woken up. I proceeded to tell Annie she was wrong that I had definitely locked everything up. But she shook her head and grinned, adamant she was right and I was wrong.

Going into my work room, I checked the windows. They were locked. I checked the front door. Locked. By this time, I rolled my eyes at Annie as much as to say, *See, you're wrong!* But she still continued to grin. Which I can tell you didn't help my grumpy attitude, but just to appease her I checked the back door and it was also locked.

I began to go upstairs, saying, 'This isn't funny, Annie. I have to work tomorrow.'

I was now positive she was just playing with me for her own entertainment.

Two steps up and I heard her say, 'Luvvy it's not safe. Check the house.'

'Oh, for God's sake, Annie, you're driving me insane!' But then I stopped and I thought, what does she mean? She has never woken me up for no good reason.

I decided to go outside and check. I wasn't actually even sure of what I was checking on, but my intuition guided me. Low and behold, one of the roller doors had been left open!

Annie was laughing, saying, 'See, Luvvy, see.'

I had not considered she now saw the new roller doors as her area of security management. I put my hand to my head, realising she was always going to be right. I turned to her and thanked her. I really should have known better than to question her security management. Thankfully she didn't say, 'I told you so, Luvvy.'

Rusty has only had one run-in with Annie. That incident occurred when I travelled back to the Solomon Islands. One night he was in bed and heard a loud crash downstairs in my meditation room. He got up to see what the noise was and found one of his stone statues on the floor. He stood there looking at the shattered statue, trying to work out how it had fallen off the bench. It was quite heavy and there was no way it could have just toppled off by itself. Then he remembered Annie! So, he went around checking the windows and doors. And sure enough, the back sliding door hadn't been locked.

Annie had most likely realised Rusty wouldn't be able to hear her words. So, she decided on another course of action to make sure the house was safe. I had to laugh at the fact she picked the heaviest statue to make her message heard. The fact that she hadn't touched any of my ornaments also made me laugh, because there are a number of those that she could have picked.

Annie is quieter these days, but I still hear from her now and again. Sometimes it's just to let me know she's there or to say good morning. She always comes forward with a grin on her face, calling me 'Luvvy.' I think our spirit security guard is pretty darn special.

I said earlier I have an on/off button I use to ensure boundaries are kept, so I can live somewhat of a normal life. But there are many times when I just intuitively know something about what others may be doing, especially those I'm close to. There are times I may text someone to check on them, only to find that the person is up to something I may have warned them against doing. This usually does freaks them out, just a little.

One night I texted a friend to see how she was doing now that she was single.

She immediately replied, 'Bloody hell woman. I was sitting here thinking I might download a dating app, just to have a look. And all that was going through my mind was your voice saying dating apps weren't a good idea. Then your text came through.'

I laughed and wrote back, 'Sometimes I'm kind of creepy, hey?'

'YES! But only sometimes.'

'Yep, sometimes I even creep myself out!'

When I look at myself, I do concede I do have a few weird, quirky traits that would seem a little unusual to the normal person. But hey, what is normal anyway? There's only one me and I can't be anything other than myself.

One of these weird and wonderful traits, is I tend to mix two words together, forming what I call a 'Trina' word. This happens a lot in my meditation classes and causes no end of laughter for myself and my students. I say myself, because even I get a little surprised at the 'Trina' words that actually come out of my mouth. I often say my students should make a 'Trina word' dictionary.

My partner, Rusty, has taken this to a whole different level. Once he knew this happened, he actually began writing all my mixed-up words or sayings down. I'm not sure what he's going to do with them, maybe he's thinking of writing his own book. It's probably going to be called, 'My Life Living with a Crazy Clairvoyant' or 'How to Survive Being in Love with a Clairvoyant.'

Rusty probably does get the brunt of my 'Trina' words and sayings. So, he has my blessing to divulge my words to the world. He may have to translate them though so everyone understands what I'm talking about.

One Friday evening we were sitting in front of the pizza oven outside, relaxing after a long week. We had the radio on our favourite station that tended to play our sort of music, definitely no rap music on this station. Now, Rusty is a little hard of hearing, so the music is often at a level I find a little loud. If I have had a full-on day of readings, my senses will become more sensitive to stimuli.

So, I'm sitting there relaxing, but thinking to myself the music is getting louder and louder. Which seriously it isn't, it was just my senses going on overload. After a while I'd had enough, the music was just too loud!

I turned to him and said quite strongly, 'For God's sake, Rusty, turn the music down. It's too loud for my sesame ears!'

He looked at me for a moment and I looked at him a little confused and dumbfounded. What did I just say? He began laughing and then I cracked up too. He got up to turn the music down and was still laughing his head off.

'Sweetie, I think you meant your sensitive ears, but I'll go with sesame ears if you want.'

I was laughing so hard at the fact that statement came out of my mouth I couldn't speak.

One other evening I was sitting downstairs, and as the night went on I was starting to get a little cool. I thought to myself I had better change from shorts to trousers.

Getting up, I said to Rusty, 'I'm just going upstairs to get my long shorts on.' I didn't think anything of what I had said and went upstairs to change.

I came back and Rusty touched my trousers, saying, 'So these are your long shorts, sweetie?'

I look at him a little confused, then realised what I had actually said and laughed.

'That's okay, sweetie. They are definitely longer than your shorts. But I think we call them trousers, not long shorts.' We both cracked up laughing at my new term for long pants or trousers.

Another day, we were driving in the car. I actually like the quietness of driving, especially when I'm the passenger and don't have to think. I was enjoying the warmth of the sun coming through the windows and thought how it was such a beautiful day.

But what came out of my mouth, in quite a serious way, was, 'It's such a beautiful day sweetheart, not a sky in the clouds.'

He looked at me and began chuckling. I was confused, why was he laughing?

He said, 'I think you meant "Not a cloud in the sky" sweetie.'

I started laughing and agreed as I realised what I'd actually said.

'Don't worry sweetie, I completely understood what came out of your mouth. It's a Trina saying. I'll write that down when we stop.'

That was the day I found out he had actually started writing my words and sayings down. When I asked why he did this, he replied, 'It's just so uniquely you and I laugh every time I read them. But it also reminds me of where we were when I read them again.'

So anyway, I hope his book is a success and my words always help to cheer people up. Because I do know (remember I'm clairvoyant) no matter how hard I try, I'm never going to stop those weird words and sayings coming out of my mouth.

No, living with the dead isn't always serious. In fact, my guides in spirit are often a cause of laughter throughout my day. People have this weird idea that spirit guides are always serious and are there only to guide and teach. I can tell you that's definitely not the case with a few of my guides. Oringo is definitely a source of laughter on many occasions throughout my days. All of my guides have their own personality, just like those of us who are still living. Yes, some are more comical than others, but I know they all like us to laugh.

Finding laughter in your day is definitely an important soul lesson. Laughter brings in happy hormones like dopamine and that results in feelings of wellbeing, reducing depression and anxiety. I think experiencing joy each day is a must and helps create a healthy balanced life.

Yes, there will be times throughout your life when laughter can be difficult to find. Times when life seems to be at its lowest and everything seems so dreary and hard. In those times, remember to find people and experiences that can add a little laughter, because your mind, body and spirit will benefit.

Be willing to laugh at yourself. This includes all those little unique quirky things you personally do that essentially makes you who you are. Try not to take life and self too seriously all the time. Find joy and laughter wherever you can, because that in itself is a life lesson well worth mastering.

Chapter Thirteen

MY PEOPLE IN SPIRIT

We are the people of the sky, the ones of Spirit.
We are your angels, guides and ancestors.
Our world is so different from yours, be still and feel it.

You sometimes speak to us in your mind and feel us in your heart.
We watch you wait for signs to be given.
We feel your pain and sorrow that we are now apart.

But we are not far away, a memory, a tear,
a thought that brings a smile.
A reminder of days gone by to be cherished.
We whisper our words within your sweet ear and
sit with you for a while.

No, you cannot touch us as you once did,
we are no longer blood and flesh.
But we do live on in our world, this we do assure.
No longer burdened by our trials on Earth, we are now born afresh.

We now move between two worlds, not a care or worry.
Love has bound us together for all time.
But we must wait until it is your time to be reunited, there is no hurry.

The world of spirit is filled with such love and joy.
We will reach for your hand when the time is right.
Then we will be together reunited in Spirit's world for evermore.

We watch from above
Often walking by your side each day
Our only wish is to embrace you with our love.

Our Little One has chosen to allow us to speak.

What is it we wish to tell you? Well, we have many wisdoms to convey. But the ultimate wisdom will always be: *you are loved*. You are loved beyond the words and feelings your world can express. This will always be the one ultimate wisdom we wish to teach and for you to learn.

We watch with love in our hearts as your world creates fear and negative thinking. And we say: do not fear, do not become negative and despondent. Look for the people and places in your world who teach love and acceptance of all who grace your earth.

See your differences as teachings of love and heed the wisdoms each difference can teach. Your differences make up your world and will always create an opportunity for soul's growth and learning. Whether that be at an individual level or a world level.

Yes, your world has failings. But it also holds such beauty and wonderment. Look for these things within self and others. Look for these things in the forests, the deserts, the mountains, the rivers, the oceans. Look for these things in the seemingly mundane. For there is much beauty, joy and wonderment that is present that you choose not to discover.

Look within and discover who you truly are. And when that is ascertained, discover who it is you wish to truly become. Our Little One has discovered truths about herself, both positive and negative, and some truths she is still learning. This is the journey of being human, the learning will always continue until your last breath from this world you call Earth. But, she has done this with great effort and taken herself out of her place of comfort to do so. By doing this, she has allowed herself to rise above what her constraints of the mind told her she was. And she still will have much work to do, but she knows this.

My People in Spirit

Within each moment you walk the earth, there is a beauty and wisdom that can be discovered if you wish to take the time. We watch with some amusement, but also much compassion as you sometimes struggle with the boredom that you think life can become. We ask you, why is this so? Why is there a feeling of there should be more? When this feeling arises, as it will, we ask you to step out into your world and go discover the simple wonderment of all that is.

What does this mean, we hear you ask? Take a step outside and look at all that surrounds you. Sit in nature, just as our friend Oringo teaches our Little One, and see with eyes that are fresh. Open your heart and mind to what you can discover. Have you ever really looked at a flower and seen every element of its beauty? Have you watched as a butterfly or dragonfly soars through the air and really seen these creatures? Or followed the marching of an ant colony as they go about their work? Or listened to the different calls of our winged friends, the birds?

All these things, although seemingly simple and mundane, can lift a soul and heal the want inside your mind.

We see each person wonder why they are here and what they should be doing. The simple answer to that question is: to live! But to truly live, first you must be present in each moment of your life.

Yes, we understand your world talks of the need for money and material things. And yes, these can be necessary in your world. But can you take these things with you when you come to our world? Of course, the answer is no! We do not judge you on what you possess when you enter our world. These material things become of little importance to yourself and those in spirit. We will ask you how have you lived. What was it that made you want to live? What made your heart fill with love for self and others?

There are times we see you weary and growing despondent with all you have to deal with in your life. In these times when the world seems to weigh heavy on your shoulders, we in spirit come closer. We whisper gently words of encouragement. We try to show you different paths that are there for you to follow. And we do this in many ways, words, feelings, dreams, synchronicities and inspiring ideas that seem to come to you out of the ether. These are just a few of the ways we guide you along your path.

We can never tell you what to do – it is our way – we can only guide, support, motivate or suggest. Ultimately, it is you that must choose what path you will follow. But we will always be by your side to help you discover what living really means. And of course, we join in on celebrating your joys, those times when the body, mind and soul feels such elation and love. These times we too feel what you experience, just as we do when you find times are challenging.

We do not judge. In our world, we have learned the wisdom of knowing a soul holds many lessons. And these can only be completed by each individual in their own time, without interference from Spirit.

We do not dismiss or berate for making choices that hinder your soul's progress. This is not our way or desire. But, we will show you at the ending of your days on Earth when you have entered our world, how different choices can lead to different paths. You will always be embraced by the love of Spirit, even if your choices have been undesirable or wrong. We understand it will be difficult for you to fully understand what we express. But we wish to convey to you our world is one of love. It is not filled with hate and judgement. We wish only for each soul to evolve so it experiences what unconditional love truly means.

There are so many of us here in spirit. Some hold great wisdom and remind even those of us that guide, how much there is for a soul to learn even in one day on your earth.

There are also many in our world that are still learning and trying to understand the meaning of a person's freewill. To experience life – to decide actions – and then to accept the consequences of those actions taken. This is a big responsibility.

We often feel your hesitation and your pleas to us in spirit to tell you what it is you need to do for your actions to be the correct actions. Again, we can guide, but we cannot decide for you, as this would mean you are not living your life and hence learning from that life.

Many years ago, our Little One was shocked by a man of the cloth, a religious man on your earth, who talked of fear and persecution. We watched as her energy began to shrink and feel threatened in a place she had felt peace when she walked through its doors. Our Little One had only experienced the feeling of love and acceptance from our world up until this point and we felt her fear and confusion.

We whispered in her ear, 'Little One, this we know not to be true,' and looked in her eyes and showed her our love. Once again, she felt the love she was accustomed to and her energy softened.

We chuckled a little because it was with the innocence of a child when she asked, 'What's wrong with him? He's so angry.'

Our Little One does not remember the time afterwards when we, her guides, sat with her and explained how this man's heaven and hell was very different to our world in spirit, and the reasons why he chose to talk this way from his church pulpit.

Yes, our world holds many different levels of souls. Some of these levels are difficult to fathom, and some levels are most definitely easier to contend with than others. But, these levels are not based on punishment and fiery pits. These are souls, who, through their own choices have to deal with the consequences of their own actions. These souls will still be able to reach for our light and feel the compassion and love we offer. But even in our world of spirit, the soul continues to learn and this will always be so, for infinity.

We watch your world change, so rapidly, without understanding the consequences of these developments. Your world has always undergone change. This is the nature of your world. Some changes have been positive and some have been negative and often destructive. We see the divisions being created by these changes. We encourage you all to let go of fear and believe more deeply in the wonderment of your world, the earth and its teachings.

We wish to talk of humility within humanity. This is something we feel that has been lost. To be humble in all things is not to be weak. When the world is humble and comes back to its origins, it listens to the needs of the universe, the world and its inhabitants. But your world strives to be more, to have more, without understanding the consequences. This need is driven by power at its most negative state. It allows you to lose an important aspect of the human form – its need to connect and be loved.

Yes, there are forces that wish to divide and conquer. These forces that do not have the desire to understand and can step forward and also destroy all that is necessary in your world. At times, your world shows us here in spirit how fragile your foundations are, because often they are built on need, desire and control.

Your world races to compete against itself. It strives for more, it strives for power. But do not despair. We ask you not to be fearful. Look to those who walk your world in a simple way, a humble way. Those who listen to Earth's beat, its heart.

Those who listen to the beat of the earth and know what time a bush blooms with the first buds of food. Those that know the sun will thaw the mountain snow and allow the streams to fill with the purest water. Their humble nature knows it is not necessary to take more than they need. For they do not fear what is to come.

Yes, even with these humble people, there is some uncertainty for the future. But they have faith that the universe and its earth will continue and provide for them if they walk their path softly, so as not to disturb the earth and what it can provide.

To stand in one's power is necessary. It creates strength when walking your path. But remember, there is no greater power than love. There is no greater power in knowing when the earth is speaking and it is time to listen. Your earth listens to you and provides all you need.

Remember, your earth can only listen to man's wants, needs and power to control for so long before it must speak strongly. Then it must show man truly he has no control. The universe, your world and other worlds must exist in unison, knowing how to be humble and grateful for all it has been given.

Do not fear your world and its wrongdoers, for in doing so, you give this negative energy more power. Instead, unite in a positive manner. Lead by example. Be with the simple way of living. There is no need for crusades and uprisings. We ask you to look firstly at your own world, yourself and your home. Let go of the need to have more than you could possibly use.

Help your earth replenish. But start doing this with yourself. Sleep when you need. Eat only when you are hungry. Drink the clearest water. Clothe yourself with comfort. Let go of the fear that resides within. Breathe and remember each day holds wonderment. This is a lesson the soul yearns for you to learn.

We ask you to remember, each one that walks your earth has those in spirit that wish to help and encourage, as much as we can and you allow. Angels, guides, relatives and others, all wish you to be happy and find peace as you walk your path through this life and those you will continue to live in the future.

Our Little One found from an early age her 'people in spirit' as she calls us have always been there for her and she has great trust in our workings. She, like many, does not always adhere to what we wish for her to explore or learn. Sometimes we do smile with compassion at her stubbornness and independence, knowing these traits can sometimes be her downfall. But that does not mean we step away from her due to her using her free will. It will just mean her choices lead her onto different pathways.

No matter what choice she makes or what path she may take, we will be standing with our Little One. No, as she has discovered, much to her dismay, not always will she have the choice of which of us in spirit stands with her. And this lesson was to be one of her greatest soul lessons. But it was ultimately given to show her in more depth the workings of Spirit, and that no matter which of her 'people' stepped back, there was always another that would step forward.

Our Little One has never held the fear of death, as she has revered our world and found peace in our ways. But even this wonderful truth can bring lessons to her in the future. She understands the depth of grief felt when someone must walk from your world to our world. This she has experienced, many times. But, she must also understand the grief felt by others when it is her turn to travel to our world. There will be many that will feel this loss, and she is yet to understand this truth to its full soul level.

Do not fear our world, it is one of love and continuation. We ask you not to fear your world but instead see the wonderment of your world. Do not fear yourself, we ask you to remember the importance of your existence. You are unique and have been born into your world for a reason. We ask you to find the wonderment in knowing you will never be replaced. For there is only one of you and your soul wants you to acknowledge this lesson. See the wonderment in self and your existence.

Go gently now and live your life fully, knowing you are loved unconditionally by those of us who reside in the world of spirit.

I thought it was important to allow my guides to have a say within this book. They always have the most beautiful words and ways of expressing life and all its ups and downs. How do I do this? It's done through automatic writing, which I have been doing for many years.

Automatic writing can be done in many ways by different individuals. The way I experience automatic writing is somewhat like dictation. I sit in meditation and allow my mind to become silent and have pen and paper on my lap. With my eyes closed, I then wait until I feel my guides come very close. I listen to their words, pick up my pen and write them down. It's as simple as that!

This is all done with my eyes shut. The words come very quickly and the writing looks very different to my own normal handwriting. Because the words do come so quickly I don't usually know what is being written on the page. That may seem odd, so I'll try and explain.

Even though I'm listening to the words, there is a level of detachment that occurs in this process. So, I detach from the word's meanings and basically go into an automatic pilot state. Once my guides have finished talking or 'dictating' to me, I open my eyes and then read their words.

I often use the process of automatic writing when I need to know something. An example of this would be if I was travelling to another country. I would sit with my guides to do automatic writing to find out if there is anything I needed to be aware of while travelling. Of course, I won't always be given every detail of the trip, but they will make me aware of certain things. Often, I won't be privy to information if there is a lesson that needs to be learned, as the information may then change how I learn the lesson.

Automatic writing is often used a lot on my silent retreats. It is a way for my guides to show me a past life or something they wish to teach me. My guides show me a lot of detail within the visions I see when working with me on retreat. There's no way I could retain the amount of information and completely understand what they were bringing to my attention if I didn't do this process. Although I don't always use automatic writing on retreat. Say, for example, if I was working with Oringo out in the forest, then I don't use automatic writing. I must come back and write what I remember and if there is anything missed. My guides will then fill in the details through images, words and feelings given in meditation or automatic writing.

I hope you find peace in my guides' words, and know their world is indeed a world of love and soul progression.

Chapter Fourteen

LESSONS TO LEARN

Here I stand on this earth, trying to master my path.
A moment, an experience, each day brings a lesson.
I know my time here is a place to learn, as I look at the aftermath.

There are times when I learn with joy and such gusto,
Applauding the fact, I have seen what is needed.
And yet other times, I feel as a student I still have so far to go.

I know our life is truly just for living.
Yes, lessons aplenty abound each day.
Yet, I know my soul is loving and forgiving.

So, I will go and travel my journey as a student of this earth.
Trying my best to master the lessons and its content.
Knowing one of these soul lessons is to always know my own worth.

I am sixty-three this year. The same age as my mother was when she took her last breath and stepped into a world I am very comfortable in, the world of spirit. As I write this book and look back over my life thus far, I see there are many, many lessons that have come my way. Some I have mastered, and I have failed miserably to learn.

I often hear people say to me, 'You are so lucky, having your guides at your side to help you through your life.'

And yes, I know without a doubt I'm extremely blessed to have my beloved guides at my side each day. But please remember, they cannot make me learn a lesson the soul has presented to me. Even with my guides giving me hints, seriously readers, I actually can be a very slow learner at times.

I agree with my guide who mentioned my stubbornness and independence being my downfall at times. I would add my lack of patience in some areas is also something I have to work on as my days turn into years.

I think about one lesson my guides taught me many years ago, that has always stayed in my mind. This lesson was learned by a simple statement they had said, after a day where I had not only failed to use patience, and my stubbornness and independence reared their heads. I was going over the day's events, berating myself because I knew I had done the wrong thing.

Claire and My Indian stepped forward and put their hands on my shoulders, saying gently, 'Little One, we will do better tomorrow.'

I knew they were agreeing that I hadn't made the wisest decisions that day. But they were also saying it was no good being so hard on myself for being human and making mistakes. Yes, that's another lesson I need to learn at some stage to not be so hard on myself. But I think we all need to work on that lesson, don't we?

My guides showed me, that no matter what lessons we don't master on any one given day, week, year or even in a lifetime, that those in spirit will still stand by our side. They love us and know the wisdom that a soul resides within a human body that holds many imperfections. As humans, we can only do our best to learn the lessons that come our way. Not all lessons will be mastered immediately. Some may even take lifetimes to understand and learn completely.

They also showed me that when I berate myself and tell myself how bad I am for not doing the right thing, I cause more soul lessons to come my way to be looked at and studied. Sometimes us humans can be our own worst enemies, can't we? We must learn at some point to forgive ourselves and understand there is always an opportunity to do better.

Throughout my life, my guides have never berated or caused me to feel less. They have only ever been supportive and loving with their Little One. And I don't want to even imagine my life without them. Because seriously they have definitely got their Little One out of some sticky situations. No, they can't make me do anything or change the lessons I need to learn. But they have guided me in ways that allow me to keep living my life. They have taught me to appreciate that even on those hard days, I'm still breathing. And that is a blessing that must be appreciated, every single day.

On one of my forest walks with Oringo, I was getting confused, losing my way because fear had filled my mind. For a moment, I had disregarded that Oringo knew his forest world and his Little One so very well. He had always told me to trust him in his forest world because he would never let anything harm me. But this forest had a different energy from what I was used to and I found myself feeling fearful and confused. I began darting here and there, not knowing which way to go – I was definitely walking like an elephant! – maybe even a stampeding one!

Eventually, I stopped. I turned to Oringo and said, 'I don't know where I am.'

I was exhausted as I'd been up since four-thirty in the morning. I was also a little annoyed at myself for not taking notice of where the sun was when I entered the forest, or landmarks that would show me the way out.

Oringo replied gently, 'Then tell me, why is it I am following you, Little One and you are not following Oringo?'

I hung my head feeling ashamed. I had disregarded him and the fact the man I knew would never allow harm to come to me, because of fear.

He smiled and said, 'Come. We will go home now, Little One. You are tired.'

Oringo proceeded to walk in front of me and show me the way out. As I followed, I reflected on how I had acted. I think he had sensed how hard I was being on myself and on the way out, he stopped abruptly at a rocky outcrop.

I was a little startled at his quick halt, but he turned to me and said, 'Look, Little One, this rock is you.'

I looked to where he was pointing and focused on the shape and markings of the large rock. I thought he must have decided we were still working, and focused all my energy on seeing what he was showing me. I looked closely at every detail of the rock and was a little dumbfounded. But then I began to chuckle at his wicked sense of humour. The large rock looked exactly like a baby elephant! Oringo was making sure his Little One wasn't becoming too hard on herself and wanted to uplift my energy.

He grinned widely as he said, 'Come, Little One, you must take photo of this rock that is you. Shame I cannot take photo of you both together.'

And yes, I did take a photo of the baby elephant rock. Every time I look at this photo I chuckle and think maybe 'My People' might have to start calling me 'Little Elephant.'

Back at the retreat house, I sat down with a cup of tea, completely exhausted. My ego was a little deflated due to the fact I had failed to trust a man I love dearly. I began to apologise to Oringo for my failure.

He came to my side and pointed to the sky. 'Little One, look, your bird family is coming to make you feel better.'

I looked up and in flew three little butcher birds who immediately came to my side. One female and two males. The female actually sitting on my leg and the other two watched from the table.

'These are smaller versions of your family. You did not fail Oringo, Little One. We will walk tomorrow at one and we will do better. But now, rest with your family. Your body and mind are weary.'

Oh, how I felt so much love and appreciation in my heart at that moment for this man and the thoughtful gift he had just given his Little One.

I learned a very valuable lesson that day. Even when you know in your heart that you can trust you are in safe hands, fear can still invade your mind. It can make your path change and become chaotic. Fear can also come from a past you have not fully healed. That day I understood how often our life experiences can create patterns that may no longer serve us. If we choose to ignore or deny those patterns, we will never completely heal. These patterns must be looked at more deeply. We must ask why they surface, in order to fully understand the lesson our soul is trying to teach us.

I will say though, the next day Oringo commended me on not walking like an elephant, which made me very pleased. I actually patted this Little One on the back for making progress with her forest teachings.

The three butcher birds stayed with me for the entire retreat, often calling me out onto the deck to spend time with them. If I happened to leave the door open they would fly into the house, curious to see what I was doing. The female often sat on top of my laptop, watching me intently as I typed. As I started to write the very beginnings of this book, it seemed as though she was there to encourage me to write my story and I appreciated her presence.

I have not mastered all of the life lessons that have been sent my way. And like all those who are reading this book I often wonder if I ever will! I keep saying to my meditation students I'm pretty sure I'll be returning to this earth. I'll need to learn all those lessons that I failed to master, or the ones I somehow dodged through using my stubborn, impatient, independent free will. But I do not fear my soul's lessons. Like you, I'm trying to do the best I can do. Well, most days anyway.

We are all guilty of being downright human. We don't always act as a compassionate, loving human being as we go through life. There will be times you dismiss your parent's advice, even when you know they are right. Times when you fall in love and hurt those who love you dearly. There will be times when anger doesn't allow forgiveness. Times when you allow excesses to enter your body and ruin your health. Times when you don't stand up and help others when you should. Times when you will act with malice. Times when you just don't like yourself and the things you may have done in the past. But, hey. You're human and so am I. We aren't perfect. We can't be perfect. We are human beings living a human experience.

When you think about all those things you could have done differently, please remember my guides' words of wisdom: 'We will do better tomorrow.' Then make a conscious effort to do just that.

A number of years ago, one of my meditation students said to me, 'Wouldn't it be easier if we didn't know all this lesson stuff?'

Because seriously, it means we have to take responsibility for our actions. What we do with our life becomes a bit more intense, because we have to take personal responsibility instead of blaming the universe and anyone else for how our life has turned out.

I agree it certainly would be easier to just go about life in a state of ignorance or denial. But I think doing that would take away a lot of the depth that life holds.

I always remember this quote: 'If you know better, then you do better.'

And I agree. Once you understand you are a soul living a human existence within the constraints of a human body and world, you become more open to trying to work out why you are here and how you can become the best version of yourself. I think that's a worthwhile lesson to study.

Do not fear the lessons you have been given to experience here on Earth. These lessons often become your reason for living and grasping life enthusiastically with both hands. It's often the motivation for getting up each day and seeing the beauty and wonder that is our world.

And on those days when life's lessons seem too hard to even contemplate, know that it's okay to stop and rest.

Say to yourself, 'Tomorrow is another day and I will do better.'

You might feel like a kindergartener, fumbling with the simplest lesson. Or you might have mastered an area of study, like a professor. Or even a student who now feels they have been put in detention. And seriously, don't we all feel like that some days?

No matter what, please know that you are loved by those in spirit in a way you have never experienced on Earth. It is necessary for you to learn to be gentle and compassionate with yourself as you go along your journey.

Yes, I know I've just pinpointed another lesson for you to study, and speaking from experience, it can be a hard one to master. But students do get holidays, even when the lessons are soul lessons. So, remember to take time in your life to just BE. Don't be afraid to laugh at your mistakes. Understand your humanness can sometimes make you feel like you are the class dunce. But Spirit doesn't see you this way and neither should you, so be gentle with yourself.

As I come to the end of writing this book, I've asked myself why I wanted to write about soul lessons. We all go through these life lessons, whether they be good or bad, joyful or sad. I had to step away for a moment to reflect on my answer.

When I started this book, I just started writing, as I often do. I didn't really have a clear direction of where I was taking the concept of this book. I knew I wanted to write about my experiences with Spirit and the experiences of my clients, but I needed to contemplate how it evolved into writing about soul lessons.

As I sat in my meditation chair and reflected on my reasons, a song came on my Spotify mix. It was a song that had played on a silent retreat I went on a couple of years ago. It was then followed by another song that I also played many times on that same retreat. The songs were from 'Lullabies for the Soul' and both resonated with me deeply and still do. Both songs speak of working in harmony with the universe and how when we allow the skies to open up and see the universe truly as it is, a light touches our heart. Beauty and love shine through. It sings of the light flowing through our tears and touching who we truly are, if we listen to our soul's wisdom.

The soul tells us the truth and if we listen with open hearts, it will tell us where we belong. Both songs sing of how the soul tells the truth without the need to hold fear. When we understand this, we spread our wings and fly. When we allow ourselves to listen to that truth, we are in harmony and fall into the universal symphonies. We become who we should be, the truest version of ourselves. Then, and only then, do we fall gently into all that is life itself. And we are in harmony with its universal symphonies.

How does that all relate to my book? One of the greatest lessons I have learned over my sixty-three years on this earth, is I can be no one but myself! Once I learned this truth, through the death of my father and many other lessons I came up against, my life held meaning. It felt like I was always meant to be here and go through what I have. Enduring sometimes hard lessons, but also, so many wonderful and joyful lessons. In simple terms, my life made sense. It doesn't mean I then saw my life becoming a bed of roses. Everything didn't just become easy in my life! But with the help of My People in spirit, it all made sense.

My People in spirit have always showed me that there is a higher hand guiding us along our journey and that the world of spirit truly exists. This, I have never had any doubt. But the people I have encountered throughout my journey, and their experiences, have also continued to show me we are always guided by a higher power. This sometimes seems like the universe is orchestrating a symphony. And once we are in tune with our soul and its lessons, we create a harmony that delivers contentment to all who are willing to hear its song.

The beautiful clients that allowed me to write of their stories have been through so much, and I have so much admiration for each person. Like myself, they are not people who are perfect. They have discovered through their own lessons in life how fragile and fleeting life can be. Through experiencing their difficult times, they have then chosen to try and understand the workings of the universe. I know this hasn't been an easy process for them, and it has taken some of them a number of years to heal. Some are maybe still in need of healing. But as they have travelled along their path, I know they have gained a deeper appreciation for life itself.

Remember, to love and be loved is the most precious gift to experience in life.

The most important lesson you will ever learn, is to live fully in your own unique way and love deeply – not only others, but also yourself. I hope the soul lessons I have written about in this book are learned easily by each and every one who reads my words.

It's funny, I'm sitting here thinking about how I should end this book. I have tried a number of endings but they didn't seem to be enough or sit well with me. Yep, there's another soul lesson. My perfectionism rearing its head and causing me problems. I promise I will study that more intently when I finish this darn book!

But as I stood up feeling a little frustrated, Claire came to my side. Smiling, she touched my shoulder and showed me a vision of a full orchestra in all its glory. The musicians watching and understanding the movements of the conductor, working together to create the most beautiful piece of music.

Then she said, 'Write what you see, my Little One.'

As I watched the vision, a piece of music came on and I listened intently to all the different instruments. I watched as the conductor interacted with each musician, showing them when to put light and shade into the piece they were playing. How he encouraged them to play with more passion or to use a gentler touch. I watched as the musicians played their instruments and thought of the many years it must have taken to master each instrument. How there would be musicians that come and go within an orchestra and each one would bring something different to the music.

Some instruments at first glance will not seem as important as others, but this is not necessarily the case. Because if we leave out one single instrument, the symphony will not sound the same. It will be incomplete. But ultimately, in order to work together, the orchestra will have to learn to understand each other, their instrument and the conductor. And when they can learn to do this, a beautiful symphony plays out into the world. It sounds so wonderful and unique that everyone stops to appreciate how it resonates with them.

I think my beautiful guide Claire was showing me we are all musicians in the orchestra of our life. Those instruments we pick up are often the lessons our soul wants us to learn. Some are very easy to master and others are more difficult.

We need to learn to take notice of the direction the conductor shows us – our guides and higher power being our conductor in life. Then we can understand an instrument can play so many different tunes.

We are so much more than what we perceive ourselves to be, if we just learn to understand our soul's intricacies.

We soon become aware of the many layers to life, just as a piece of music or symphony has so many layers if we only choose to stop and truly listen. And in understanding this, we can come together. Conductor, musician, instrument and music, all working together to create a beautiful sound that is truly unique – because it is the symphony of your life.

My wish for you all reading this book is that you always are in tune with your soul.

Hear the harmony created by the universe and your higher power.

Believe in the workings of a spiritual force that is focused solely on love.

Understand this beautiful energy is helping you each day to return to who you truly are and discover all you can truly be in the future.

Know deep within your heart you are always being divinely guided each and every day by a loving and compassionate hand. And in doing so, I know you will become the most beautiful symphony.

This energy sings of peace and contentment. It can be felt by everyone you come into contact with as you walk your path. It spreads out to the world and all who need to feel its powerful vibration.

But most of all, it allows you to understand when you work with your soul you are creating your own unique symphony. That unique piece of music will always become the most beautiful masterpiece. You will be in harmony with yourself, life and the universal energy of your soul.

About the Author

Trina Brown is a clairvoyant medium, healer, meditation teacher and the author of *Clairvoyant Amongst the Coconuts*. She has interacted with Spirit since she was a child and is able to pass on messages from loved ones in spirit and support clients on their healing journey. Trina has been working in the spiritual field for over thirty-five years.

She often combines her abilities to create immersive retreats and workshops. These experiences help her clients delve deeper into who they are and discover how to become the best version of themselves. As a reader, Trina is known as being straight to the point but compassionate. She often adds her own unique sense of humour when needed.

One of Trina's favourite quotes is, 'Remember to laugh often, it's good for the soul.'

She is a mother of two and Gram to three beautiful grandchildren. Trina loves musical theatre, reading, and travelling – often returning to her other island home the Solomon Islands. Trina resides in Redcliffe, Queensland with her partner.

If you would like to know more about her body of work, visit her website:

www.trinabrownclairvoyant.com.au

Previous books by
Trina Brown

Clairvoyant
amongst the
Coconuts

My Journey is Your Journey

Clairvoyant Amongst the Coconuts takes you on a journey from Australia to the Solomon Islands, where Trina Brown settles in to a new way of life and makes a home away from home.

From teaching English at the community school, to adventures on the high seas and a near-miss with a boiling volcano, Trina takes you along for the ride.

With her guides in spirit leading the way, Trina shares her experience of Island life from first stepping foot off the plane, to becoming a much-loved member of the community. This heartwarming story is also about building Hope, a small school in the Solomon Islands.

But more than that, *Clairvoyant Amongst the Coconuts* is a journey into self. It is an invitation to embrace your own journey, through meditations, self-reflection exercises, and becoming more connected to your intuition.

If you are seeking answers and understanding as you navigate your own path, you will undoubtedly find Trina's journey inspirational and encouraging. Allow her to act as your guide, as she explains what it takes to discover the purpose of being, and the need for Hope.

Clairvoyant Amongst the Coconuts will show you anything is possible if you have Hope in your heart and take life one step at a time.

www.ingramcontent.com/pod-product-compliance
Lightning Source LLC
Chambersburg PA
CBHW041317110526
44591CB00021B/2813